Baking
Is
Fun

Volume 3

Recipes 191-270

Cover Recipe Page 54

ISBN 0-9691357-2-6

Printed and Bound in Austria

Here it is! Our very own **"Christmas Baking — Baking is Fun"** **(Volume 3)**. This volume consists of recipes for the Christmas season which over many years have helped make the special atmosphere of an Austrian, German and Swiss Christmas. Now you too can spoil your family and friends with traditional Holiday Baking!

This volume also contains a special addition — recipes for diabetics.

As always, all recipes have been tested in the **oetker** kitchens and use many **oetker** fine quality products.

Christmas is a time for sharing and doing things together — the younger members of your family will enjoy helping to make and decorate the fun recipes: build a gingerbread house, make a Christmas Calendar, a Santa Claus, or even a delicious chocolate train.

If you do not own volume 1 and 2 of our "Baking is Fun" series as yet — why not contact us at **oetker** in Toronto. We would like to hear from you — share your suggestions — let us know how we can help you.

Merry Christmas! Happy Holidays!

Yours sincerely,
oetker Recipe Service

Address: **oetker ltd.**
2229 Drew Road
Mississauga, Ont.
L5S 1E5

The following baking books are also available:

Baking Is Fun Volume 1, Recipes 1-93
Baking Is Fun Volume 2, Recipes 94-190

You may order each of these books at

oetker Recipe Service
2229 Drew Road
Mississauga, Ontario
L5S 1E5

Contents

OOKIES

Cinnamon Stars

Dough:

3	egg whites	3
250 g	sugar	1¼ cups
1 pkg	**oetker** vanilla sugar	1 pkg.
4-8 g	cinnamon	1-2 tsp.
350 g	ground almonds	3½ cups
	icing sugar	

PREHEAT oven to 150°C (300°F). Grease a baking sheet.
BEAT egg whites to soft peaks. Gradually add sugar and vanilla sugar, beating to stiff peaks.
SET ASIDE about 50 mL (¼ cup) egg white mixture.
FOLD cinnamon and almonds into remaining mixture.
WORK all ingredients together quickly to make a smooth dough.
ROLL out dough on surface dusted with icing sugar to 6 mm (¼″) thickness.
CUT out stars with cookie cutter rinsing it frequently in hot water.
SPREAD reserved egg white mixture on stars.
PLACE on prepared baking sheet.
BAKE on middle oven rack at 150°C (300°F) for about 20 minutes.
STORE in airtight container.
Preparation time: approx. 50 min.
Yield: 50-60 cookies

Red Currant Stars

Dough:

70 g	butter	⅓ cup
50 g	sugar	¼ cup
1 pkg	**oetker** vanilla sugar	1 pkg.
1	egg	1
2 g	cinnamon	½ tsp.
5 drops	**oetker** lemon flavouring concentrate	5 drops
50 mL	sour cream	¼ cup
280 g	all-purpose flour	1¾ cups

Decoration:

1	egg white, slightly beaten	1
50 g	icing sugar	⅓ cup
4 g	cinnamon	1 tsp.
90 mL	strained red currant jam or marmalade	⅓ cup

For Deep Frying:

oil or shortening

Dough:
CREAM butter, sugar and vanilla sugar in a mixer bowl until light and fluffy. Gradually add egg, cinnamon, flavouring concentrate and sour cream.
STIR in ¾ of flour. Mix well.
WORK in remaining flour.
CHILL for easy rolling (1 hour).
ROLL out dough on lightly floured surface to 3 mm (⅛″) thickness.
CUT out star shapes. Cut small hole in center of half the cookies using a thimble.
BRUSH with egg white and place one on top of another. Press together slightly.
HEAT fat to 190°C (375°F).
LOWER stars into fat, a few at a time.
BROWN on one side, then turn to brown on other side (3-5 minutes).
REMOVE from fat. Drain on paper towelling.
COMBINE icing sugar and cinnamon.
SPRINKLE on stars.
DECORATE with jam.
Preparation time: approx. 60 min.
Yield: 30-40 cookies

Fruit Squares

Dough:

4	egg yolks	4
250 g	sugar	1¼ cups
1 pkg	**oetker** vanilla sugar	1 pkg.
125 mL	water	½ cup
125 mL	vegetable oil	½ cup
50 g	raisins	½ cup
100 g	chopped nuts	¾ cup
100 g	semi-sweet chocolate, chopped	4 sq.
50 g	chopped candied orange peel	½ cup
50 g	chopped candied lemon peel	½ cup
4	egg whites	4
300 g	all-purpose flour	2 cups
8 g	**oetker** baking powder	2 tsp.

Dough:
PREHEAT oven to 180°C (350°F). Grease a 2 L (39 cm × 26 cm/15" × 10") jelly roll pan.
COMBINE egg yolks, ⅔ of sugar and vanilla sugar in mixer bowl. Gradually add water and oil. Beat at high speed of electric mixer until thick and creamy.
ADD raisins, nuts, chocolate, orange and lemon peel to egg mixture.
BEAT egg whites to soft peaks. Gradually add remaining sugar beating to stiff peaks.
FOLD into egg yolk mixture.
SIFT flour and baking powder over egg mixture.
FOLD all ingredients together until well blended.
PRESS dough onto prepared pan.
BAKE on middle oven rack at 180°C (350°F) for 25-30 minutes.
CUT into squares while still warm.
Preparation time: approx. 50 min.
Yield: 70-80 squares

Coconut Trees

Dough:

220 g	all-purpose flour	1½ cups
4 g	**oetker** baking powder	1 tsp.
100 g	desiccated coconut	1½ cups
70 g	sugar	⅓ cup
1 pkg	**oetker** vanilla sugar	1 pkg.
1	egg	1
150 g	sweet (unsalted) butter, cold	¾ cup

Glaze:

1 pkg	**oetker** Chocofix OR	1 pkg.
100 g	semi-sweet chocolate	4 sq.
50 g	sweet (unsalted) butter	¼ cup

Decoration:

75 mL	strained red currant jam or marmalade icing sugar or shredded coconut	5 tbsp.

Dough:
PREHEAT oven to 160°C (325°F). Grease two baking sheets.
COMBINE flour and baking powder together on pastry board. Make a well in centre.
PUT coconut, sugar, vanilla sugar and egg in well. Work a little of dry ingredients into egg mixture.
CUT cold butter into small pieces over flour mixture.
WORK all ingredients together quickly to make a smooth dough.
CHILL for easy rolling (1 hour).
ROLL out dough on floured surface to 3 mm (⅛") thickness.
CUT into star shapes. For each cookie cut 3 large and 1 small star.
PLACE on prepared baking sheets using separate baking sheets for the two sizes of stars.
BAKE on middle oven rack at 160°C (325°F), large stars for 8-10 minutes, small stars for 4-5 minutes.
Glaze:
SOFTEN Chocofix as directed on package
OR
COMBINE chocolate and butter in top of double boiler. Place over boiling water, stirring until smoothly melted.
SPREAD jam on ⅓ of large stars.
COVER with other ⅓ of large stars, spread again with jam and cover with remaining ⅓ of large stars, forming tree shape.
SPREAD jam in center of top stars and cover with small size stars.
DECORATE with glaze, icing sugar or coconut.
Preparation time: approx. 60 min.
Yield: 20-30 cookies

Chocolate Pretzels

Dough:

200 g	sweet (unsalted) butter	1	cup
120 g	sugar	⅔	cup
1 pkg	**oetker** vanilla sugar	1	pkg.
1	egg	1	
1	egg yolk	1	
1 btl	**oetker** rum flavouring concentrate	1	btl.
300 g	all-purpose flour	2	cups

Glaze:

1 pkg	**oetker** Chocofix OR	1	pkg.
100 g	semi-sweet chocolate	4	sq.
50 g	sweet (unsalted) butter	¼	cup

Dough:
PREHEAT oven to 160°C (325°F). Grease a baking sheet.
CREAM butter, sugar and vanilla sugar in mixer bowl until light and fluffy. Gradually add egg, egg yolk and flavouring concentrate. Stir in flour, mixing well.
PUT dough into decorating bag with round tube.
SQUEEZE onto prepared baking sheet in small pretzels.
BAKE on middle oven rack at 160°C (325°F) for 10-15 minutes.

Chocolate Glaze:
SOFTEN Chocofix as directed on package
OR
COMBINE chocolate and butter in top of double boiler.
PLACE over boiling water, stirring until smoothly melted.
DECORATE half or all of pretzels with chocolate glaze.
Preparation time: approx. 60 min.
Yield: 70-80 cookies

Chocolate Nut Strips

Dough:

130 g	sweet (unsalted) butter	⅔	cup
130 g	sugar	⅔	cup
1 pkg	**oetker** vanilla sugar	1	pkg.
3	egg yolks	3	
130 g	all-purpose flour	¾	cup
4 g	**oetker** baking powder	1	tsp.
130 g	chocolate chips	¾	cup
80 g	ground nuts	¾	cup
3	egg whites	3	

Decoration:

100 g	chopped nuts	1	cup

Dough:
PREHEAT oven to 180°C (350°F). Grease a 2 L (39 cm × 26 cm/15″ × 10″) jelly roll pan and line with waxed paper. Grease again.
CREAM butter, sugar, vanilla sugar and egg yolks together in mixer bowl until light and fluffy.
SIFT flour and baking powder together over creamed mixture. Mix well.
STIR in chocolate chips and nuts.
BEAT egg whites to stiff peaks.
FOLD into creamed mixture.
TURN batter into prepared pan.
SPRINKLE evenly with chopped nuts and push gently into surface of batter.
BAKE on middle oven rack at 180°C (350°F) for 25-30 minutes.
CUT into strips (5 cm × 1 cm/2″ × ½″) while warm.
Preparation time: approx. 50 min.
Yield: about 10 dozen cookies

Almond Crescents

Dough:

300 g	all-purpose flour	2	cups
100 g	ground almonds	1	cup
70 g	sugar	⅓	cup
1 pkg	**oetker** vanilla sugar	1	pkg.
250 g	butter, cold	1¼	cups

Decoration:

150 g	sifted icing sugar	1	cup
1 pkg	**oetker** vanilla sugar	1	pkg.

Dough:

PREHEAT oven to 160°C (325°F). Grease a baking sheet.
BLEND flour, almonds, sugar and vanilla sugar on a pastry board.
CUT cold butter into small pieces over dry ingredients. Work all ingredients together quickly into a smooth dough.
SHAPE dough into rolls about the size of a pencil. CUT into 5 cm (2″) pieces.
FORM into crescents on prepared baking sheet.
BAKE on middle oven rack at 160°C (325°F) for 15-20 minutes or until light golden.
ROLL warm cookies in mixture of icing sugar and vanilla sugar.
Preparation time: approx. 70 min.
Yield: 100 cookies

Red Currant Rounds

Dough:

600 g	all-purpose flour	4	cups
220 g	sugar	1	cup
2 pkg	**oetker** vanilla sugar	2	pkg.
4	egg yolks	4	
400 g	butter, cold	2	cups

Filling:

150 mL	strained red currant jam or marmalade	⅔	cup

Decoration:

	icing sugar

Dough:

PREHEAT oven to 180°C (350°F). Grease a baking sheet.
SIFT flour onto pastry board. Make a well in centre.
PUT sugar, vanilla sugar and egg yolks in well. Mix small amount of flour into centre ingredients to make a thick paste.
CUT cold butter into small pieces over flour mixture. Working quickly from the centre, work all ingredients together to make a smooth dough.
CHILL for easy rolling (½ hour).
ROLL out dough on lightly floured surface to 3 mm (⅛″) thickness.
CUT into 5 cm (2″) rounds. Cut 3 small holes with floured thimble in half the cookie rounds.
PLACE on prepared baking sheet.
BAKE on middle oven rack at 180°C (350°F) for 10-12 minutes or until light golden brown. Cool.
SPREAD jam on solid rounds. Cover with cut-out rounds.
DUST with icing sugar while cookies are still warm.
Preparation time: approx. 80 min.
Yield: 60-70 cookies

Almond Crisps

Dough:

250 g	all-purpose flour	1⅔	cups
8 g	**oetker** baking powder	2	tsp.
100 g	sugar (coarse)	½	cup
4 g	cinnamon	1	tsp.
4 g	ginger	1	tsp.
1 g	ground cloves	¼	tsp.
30 g	ground almonds	⅓	cup
1	egg	1	
120 g	butter, cold	⅔	cup

Decoration:

1	egg white, slightly beaten	1	
50 g	sliced almonds	½	cup

Dough:
PREHEAT oven to 160°C (325°F). Grease a baking sheet and line with waxed paper. Grease again.
SIFT flour and baking powder together onto pastry board. Make a well in centre.
PUT sugar, cinnamon, ginger, cloves, almonds and egg in well. Mix small amount of flour mixture into centre ingredients to make thick paste.
CUT cold butter into small pieces over flour mixture. Working quickly from the centre, work all ingredients together to make a smooth dough. If dough is sticky, chill slightly for easy handling (½ hour).
ROLL out dough on lightly floured surface to 3 mm (⅛") thickness.
CUT into 5 cm (2") rounds.
BRUSH with egg white and sprinkle with almonds.
PLACE on prepared baking sheet.
BAKE on middle oven rack at 160°C (325°F) for about 10 minutes or until light golden.
Preparation time: approx. 50 min.
Yield: 50-60 cookies

Fleurons

Pastry:

1 pkg	frozen puff pastry (4 sheets)	1	pkg.

For Brushing:

1	egg, slightly beaten	1	

Lemon Glaze:

50 g	sifted icing sugar	⅓	cup
15-30 mL	lemon juice	1-2	tbsp.

Chocolate Glaze:

1 pkg	**oetker** Chocofix OR	1	pkg.
100 g	semi-sweet chocolate	4	sq.
50 g	sweet (unsalted) butter	¼	cup

Decoration:

	coloured sugar sprinkles, optional

Pastry:
PREHEAT oven to 200°C (400°F). Moisten baking sheet.
THAW puff pastry according to package directions.
ROLL out pastry to rectangle 40 × 30 cm (16" × 14").
CUT pastry into desired shapes.
PLACE on moist baking sheet.
BRUSH with slightly beaten egg.
BAKE at 200°C (400°F) for about 10 minutes or until puffed and golden.
Lemon Glaze:
COMBINE sifted icing sugar and lemon juice to make a smooth glaze.
Chocolate Glaze:
SOFTEN Chocofix as directed on package
OR
COMBINE chocolate and butter in top of double boiler.
PLACE over boiling water, stirring until smoothly melted.
DECORATE with glazes and coloured sugar if desired.
Preparation time: approx. 60 min.
Yield: 50-60 cookies

Gingerbread Cookies

Dough:

300 g	all-purpose flour	2	cups
8 g	baking soda	2	tsp.
2 g	salt	½	tsp.
4 g	cinnamon	1	tsp.
4 g	ginger	1	tsp.
2 g	cloves	½	tsp.
250 g	brown sugar	1	cup
150 g	butter, softened	¾	cup
60 g	molasses	¼	cup
1	egg	1	

For Brushing:

1	egg, slightly beaten	1	

Decoration:

blanched almonds
candied cherries
hazelnuts
angelica

Chocolate Glaze:

2 pkg	**oetker** Chocofix	2	pkg.
	OR		
200 g	semi-sweet chocolate	8	sq.
100 g	sweet (unsalted) butter	½	cup

Lemon Glaze:

100 g	sifted icing sugar	⅔	cup
15-30 mL	lemon juice	1-2	tbsp.

Dough:
PREHEAT oven to 180°C (350°F). Grease a baking sheet.
COMBINE flour, baking soda, salt and spices.
STIR well to blend.
CREAM butter, brown sugar, molasses and egg together until light and fluffy.
ADD flour mixture to creamed mixture.
MIX well.
CHILL if necessary for easy handling (about 1 hour).
ROLL out dough on lightly floured surface to 5 mm (¼") thickness.
CUT into desired shapes with cookie cutter.
BRUSH dough with beaten egg.
DECORATE with almonds, candied cherries, hazelnut and angelica OR Glaze after baking.
BAKE on middle oven rack at 180°C (350°F) for about 10 minutes. Cool.
Chocolate Glaze:
SOFTEN Chocofix as directed on package
OR
COMBINE chocolate and butter in top of double boiler.
PLACE over boiling water, stirring until smoothly melted.
DECORATE cookies with glazes.
TIP: To use as Christmas tree decoration: Make small holes in top of cookies before baking.
Preparation time: approx. 90 min.
Yield: 40-50 cookies

Oatmeal Kisses

Dough:

30 mL	vegetable oil	2	tbsp.
120 g	rolled oats, finely ground	1¼	cups
50 g	chopped hazelnuts	½	cup
2	egg whites	2	
140 g	sugar	⅔	cup

Decoration:

whole hazelnuts

Dough:
PREHEAT oven to 150°C (300°F). Grease a baking sheet.
HEAT vegetable oil in shallow pan.
TOAST oats and nuts in oil until golden brown. Cool.
BEAT egg whites to soft peaks.
ADD sugar gradually, beating to stiff peaks.
FOLD oats and nuts into egg whites gently.
DROP by small spoonfuls onto prepared baking sheet.
DECORATE with hazelnuts, setting them firmly into dough.
BAKE on middle oven rack at 150°C (300°F) for 15-20 minutes or until light golden.
COOL before removing from pan.
Preparation time: approx. 40 min.
Yield: 50-60 cookies

Chocolate Sticks

Dough:

300 g	all-purpose flour	2 cups	
50 g	ground nuts	½ cup	
50 g	semi-sweet chocolate, grated	2 sq.	
120 g	sugar	⅔ cup	
1 pkg	**oetker** vanilla sugar	1 pkg.	
1	egg	1	
200 g	butter, cold	1 cup	

Decoration:

100 g	semi-sweet chocolate	4 sq.	
50 g	sweet (unsalted) butter	¼ cup	

Dough:

PREHEAT oven to 180°C (350°F). Grease a baking sheet.

BLEND flour, nuts and grated chocolate together on a pastry board. Make a well in centre.

PUT sugar, vanilla sugar and egg in well. Work a little of dry ingredients into egg mixture.

CUT cold butter into small pieces over flour mixture.

WORK all ingredients together quickly to make a smooth dough.

CHILL for easy rolling (½ hour).

SHAPE dough into rolls about the size of a finger.

CUT into 5 cm (2") pieces.

PLACE on prepared baking sheet.

BAKE on middle oven rack at 180°C (350°F) for 12-18 minutes or until light golden.

COOL.

Glaze:

MELT chocolate and butter together over low heat, stirring until smoothly blended.

DIP ends of cooled cookies in chocolate. Place on waxed paper to cool until chocolate is set.

Preparation time: approx. 90 min.

Yield: 100 cookies

Pistachio Stars

Dough:

400 g	all-purpose flour	2⅔ cups	
100 g	ground, toasted hazelnuts	1 cup	
120 g	sugar	⅔ cup	
1 pkg	**oetker** vanilla sugar	1 pkg.	
3 drops	**oetker** lemon flavouring concentrate	3 drops	
1	egg	1	
1	egg yolk	1	
250 g	butter, cold	1¼ cups	

Filling:

75-90 mL	strained red currant jam or marmalade	5-6 tbsp.	

Glaze:

150 g	sifted icing sugar	1⅓ cups	
1	egg white, slightly beaten	1	

Decoration:

	chopped pistachios

Dough:

PREHEAT oven to 180°C (350°F). Grease a baking sheet.

COMBINE flour and nuts together on pastry board. Make a well in centre.

PUT sugar, vanilla sugar, flavouring concentrate, egg and egg yolk in well. Work a little of dry ingredients into egg mixture.

CUT cold butter into small pieces over flour mixture.

WORK all ingredients together quickly to make a smooth dough.

CHILL for easy rolling (½ hour).

ROLL out on lightly floured surface to 3 mm (⅛") thickness.

CUT into star shapes (equal amounts of 3 different sizes).

PLACE on prepared baking sheet.

BAKE on middle oven rack at 180°C (350°F) for 7-10 minutes.

Glaze:

COMBINE sifted icing sugar and egg white to make a smooth paste.

PUT stars, one of each size together with jam. Place largest star on the bottom, then middle size then smallest star on top.

DECORATE with glaze and pistachios as desired.

Preparation time: approx. 70 min.

Yield: 40-50 cookies

Marzipan Dollars

Dough:

150 g	all-purpose flour	1	cup
2 g	**oetker** baking powder	½	tsp.
150 g	ground hazelnuts	1	cup
80 g	sugar	⅓	cup
1 pkg	**oetker** vanilla sugar	1	pkg.
30 mL	water	2	tbsp.
120 g	sweet (unsalted) butter, cold	⅔	cup

Filling:

250 g	marzipan	9	oz.
150 g	sifted icing sugar	1⅓	cups
	strained red currant jam or marmalade		

Glaze:

100 g	sifted icing sugar	1	cup
30-45 mL	lemon juice	2-3	tbsp.

Decoration:

hazelnuts
finely chopped pistachios
candied cherries
angelica
melted chocolate
pine nuts
almonds

Dough:
PREHEAT oven to 200°C (400°F). Grease a baking sheet.
COMBINE flour, baking powder and nuts together on a pastry board. Make a well in centre.
PUT sugar, vanilla sugar and water in well. Mix small amount of flour mixture into centre ingredients to make a thick paste.
CUT cold butter into small pieces over flour mixture. Working quickly from centre, work all ingredients together to make a smooth dough. If dough is sticky, chill slightly for easy handling (½ hour).
ROLL out dough on lightly floured surface to 6 mm (¼") thickness.
CUT into 5 cm (2") rounds.
PLACE on prepared baking sheet.
BAKE on middle oven rack at 200°C (400°F) for 8-10 minutes. Let cool.
Filling:
COMBINE marzipan and icing sugar.
KNEAD well until smooth and well blended.
ROLL out thinly on board dusted with icing sugar.
CUT out 5 cm (2") diameter rounds.
SPREAD jam thinly on cookies. Cover with marzipan rounds.
Glaze:
COMBINE sifted icing sugar and lemon juice to make a smooth paste.
SPREAD glaze thinly onto marzipan rounds.
DECORATE as desired.
Preparation time: approx. 90 min.
Yield: 50-60 cookies

Peanut Crunchies

Dough:

80 g	butter, softened	⅓	cup
70 g	sugar	⅓	cup
1 pkg	**oetker** vanilla sugar	1	pkg.
1	egg	1	
50 g	ground peanuts	½	cup
150 g	wholewheat flour	1	cup

Filling:

100 g	liquid honey	⅓	cup
150 g	peanuts	1½	cups

For Brushing:

1	egg, lightly beaten	1	

Dough:
PREHEAT oven to 190°C (375°F). Grease a baking sheet. Line with waxed paper. Grease again.
CREAM butter, sugar, vanilla sugar and egg together in mixer bowl.
BEAT at medium speed until light and fluffy.
FOLD in ground peanuts and ¾ of flour.
CHILL about 30 minutes for easy rolling.
MIX honey and peanuts for filling. Chill.
SHAPE dough into a roll (3 cm/1¼" diameter).
CUT into pieces 1 cm (⅓") thickness.
PRESS indentation into centre of each cookie with wooden spoon or finger.
PLACE cookies on prepared baking sheet.
BRUSH dough with lightly beaten egg.
BAKE on middle oven rack at 190°C (375°F) for 10-15 minutes. While cookies are still warm, fill centres with peanut mixture. Let cool.
Preparation time: approx. 60 min.
Yield: 30-40 cookies

Meringue Fantasies

Meringue:

3	egg whites	3
70 g	granulated sugar	⅓ cup
120 g	sifted icing sugar	1 cup

Decoration:

coloured sugar sprinkles
melted chocolate,
optional

Method:
PREHEAT oven to 70°C (150°F). Grease a baking
sheet. Line with waxed paper. Grease again.
BEAT egg whites in small mixer bowl to soft peaks.
Gradually add granulated sugar, beating until stiff and
sugar is completely dissolved.
FOLD in icing sugar thoroughly.
PUT meringue into decorating bag.
SQUEEZE desired shapes onto prepared baking sheet.
SPRINKLE with coloured sugar if desired.
BAKE on middle oven rack at 70°C (150°F) for
90-100 minutes or until dry but not brown.
DECORATE if desired with melted chocolate. Place
on waxed paper until chocolate is set.
STORE in airtight container.
Preparation time: approx. 50 min.
Yield: 40-50 meringues

Almond Macaroons

2	egg whites	2
140 g	sifted icing sugar	1 cup
250 g	ground almonds	2½ cups
2 mL	cinnamon	½ tsp.

PREHEAT oven to 150°C (300°F). Grease a baking
sheet. Line with waxed paper. Grease again.
BEAT egg whites in small mixer bowl to soft peaks.
Gradually add icing sugar, beating to stiff peaks.
COMBINE almonds and cinnamon.
FOLD into egg mixture gently.
PUT mixture into decorating bag using a large, round
icing tube. Squeeze small amounts onto prepared
baking sheet.
BAKE on middle oven rack at 150°C (300°F) for
20-25 minutes or until dry. Cool.
STORE in airtight container to mellow for
approximately 1 week before serving.
Preparation time: approx. 50 min.
Yield: 60-70 macaroons

Caraway Pretzels

Dough:

180	g	all-purpose flour	1¼	cups
	pinch	salt		pinch
1		egg yolk	1	
45	mL	sour cream	3	tbsp.
80	g	butter, cold	⅓	cup

For Brushing:

| 1 | | egg white, lightly beaten | 1 | |

Decoration:

| | | caraway seeds | | |

Method:
PREHEAT oven to 180°C (350°F). Grease a baking sheet. Line with waxed paper. Grease again.
SIFT flour and salt onto pastry board. Make a well in centre.
PUT egg yolk and sour cream in centre. Mix small amount of flour mixture into centre ingredients to make a thick paste.
CUT cold butter into small pieces over flour.
WORK all ingredients together quickly into a smooth dough.
CHILL ½ hour for easy shaping.
SHAPE dough into rolls about the size of a finger.
PLACE onto prepared baking sheet.
BRUSH with lightly beaten egg white.
SPRINKLE with caraway seeds.
BAKE on middle oven rack at 180°C (350°F) for 20-25 minutes or until light golden.
Preparation time: approx. 50 min.
Yield: 30-40 pretzels

Cheese Munchies

Dough:

150	g	all-purpose flour	1	cup
150	g	Quark or ricotta cheese	¾	cup
150	g	butter, cold	¾	cup

For Brushing:

| 1 | | egg, lightly beaten | 1 | |

Decoration:

50	g	grated Parmesan cheese	½	cup
	pinch	salt		pinch
		paprika		
		caraway seeds		

Dough:
PREHEAT oven to 200°C (400°F). Grease a baking sheet. Line with waxed paper. Grease again.
SIFT flour onto pastry board. Make a well in centre.
PUT Quark or ricotta cheese in well.
CUT cold butter into small pieces over flour.
WORK all ingredients together quickly into a smooth dough.
CHILL for about 2 hours.
ROLL out dough on lightly floured surface to 3 mm (⅛") thickness.
CUT into desired shapes.
PLACE on prepared baking sheet.
BRUSH with lightly beaten egg.
SPRINKLE lightly with Parmesan cheese, salt, paprika and caraway seeds.
BAKE on middle oven rack at 200°C (400°F) for 7-10 minutes or until light golden.
Preparation time: approx. 60 min.
Yield: 50-60 munchies

Hazelnut Sugar Wheels

Dough:

150 g	all-purpose flour	1	cup
4 g	**oetker** baking powder	1	tsp.
70 g	sugar	¼	cup
1 pkg	**oetker** vanilla sugar	1	pkg.
5 mL	cinnamon	1	tsp.
5 drops	**oetker** lemon flavouring concentrate	5	drops
80 g	ground hazelnuts	¾	cup
120 g	sweet (unsalted) butter, cold	⅔	cup

Decoration:

50 g	coarse granulated sugar	⅓	cup
75 mL	red currant jelly marmalade	⅓	cup

Method:
PREHEAT oven to 160°C (325°F). Grease a baking sheet.
SIFT flour and baking powder onto pastry board. Make a well in centre.
PUT sugar, vanilla sugar, cinnamon, flavouring concentrate and hazelnuts in well.
CUT cold butter into small pieces over flour mixture.
WORK all ingredients together quickly to make a smooth dough. Chill slightly for easy shaping (about ½ hour).
SHAPE dough into a roll 3 cm (1¼") diameter.
CUT into 5 mm (¼") thick slices.
ROLL edge in coarse sugar.
PLACE on prepared baking sheet.
PRESS indentation in centre of each cookie with finger.
FILL indentation with jam.
BAKE on middle oven rack at 160°C (325°F) for 10-15 minutes.
Preparation time: approx. 50 min.
Yield: 50-60 cookies

Pistachio Saddles

Dough:

2	eggs	2	
90 g	sugar	½	cup
1 pkg	**oetker** vanilla sugar	1	pkg.
½ btl	**oetker** almond flavouring concentrate	½	btl.
80 g	all-purpose flour	½	cup

Glaze:

2 pkg	**oetker** Chocofix OR	2	pkg.
200 g	semi-sweet chocolate	8	sq.
100 g	sweet (unsalted) butter	½	cup

Decoration:

50 g	finely chopped pistachios	½	cup

Dough:
PREHEAT oven to 160°C (325°F). Grease a baking sheet.
BEAT eggs, sugar, vanilla sugar and flavouring concentrate on high speed of electric mixer until thick and creamy.
FOLD flour into creamed mixture.
DROP mixture by small spoonfuls onto prepared baking sheet, leaving about 4 cm (1½") between each for spreading.
BAKE on middle oven rack at 160°C (325°F) for 7-10 minutes or until light golden.
WHILE still hot, place each cookie over a wooden spoon handle to make the curved shape.
COOL completely.
Decoration:
SOFTEN Chocofix as directed on package
OR
COMBINE chocolate and butter in top of double boiler.
PLACE over boiling water stirring until smoothly melted.
DECORATE cookies with glaze.
SPRINKLE with pistachios.
Preparation time: approx. 60 min.
Yield: 40-50 cookies

Chocolate Macaroons

Dough:

2	egg whites	2
140 g	sifted icing sugar	1 cup
1 pkg	**oetker** vanilla sugar	1 pkg.
100 g	semi-sweet chocolate, grated	4 sq.
150 g	ground hazelnuts	1½ cups

Glaze:

50 g	semi-sweet chocolate	2 sq.
30 g	shortening	¼ cup

Decoration:

	sliced almonds

Dough:
PREHEAT oven to 160°C (325°F). Line a baking sheet with waxed paper.
BEAT egg whites to soft peaks. Gradually add icing sugar and vanilla sugar beating to stiff peaks.
FOLD in grated chocolate and ⅔ of nuts.
KNEAD remaining nuts into mixture.
ROLL out dough on surface sprinkled with icing sugar to 6 mm (¼″) thickness.
CUT into desired shapes.
PLACE onto prepared baking sheet.
BAKE at 160°C (325°F) for 15-20 minutes.
Glaze:
COMBINE chocolate and shortening in top of double boiler.
PLACE over boiling water, stirring until smoothly melted.
DECORATE cookies with glaze.
SPRINKLE with sliced almonds.
STORE in airtight container.
Preparation time: approx. 60 min.
Yield: 50-60 macaroons

Marzipan Delights

Dough:

150 g	all-purpose flour	1 cup
30 mL	cocoa	2 tbsp.
80 g	sugar	⅓ cup
1 pkg	**oetker** vanilla sugar	1 pkg.
1	egg yolk	1
120 g	sweet (unsalted) butter, cold	⅔ cup

Filling:

120 g	marzipan	4½ oz.
50 g	sugar	¼ cup
15 mL	lemon juice	1 tbsp.

Decoration:

1 pkg	**oetker** Chocofix	1 pkg.
	OR	
100 g	semi-sweet chocolate	4 sq.
50 g	sweet (unsalted) butter	¼ cup

Dough:
PREHEAT oven to 180°C (350°F). Grease a baking sheet.
SIFT flour and cocoa together onto pastry board. Make a well in centre.
PUT sugar, vanilla sugar and egg yolk in well. Mix small amount of flour mixture into centre ingredients to make a thick paste.
CUT cold butter into small pieces over flour mixture.
Working quickly from centre, work all ingredients together to make a smooth dough. If dough is sticky, chill for easy handling (½ hour).
COMBINE marzipan, sugar and lemon juice for filling.
KNEAD well into a smooth paste.
SHAPE into a roll approximately 50 cm (19″) long.
ROLL out cookie dough on lightly floured surface.
PLACE marzipan roll on dough.
WRAP dough tightly around roll. Seal seam.
CUT into pieces 1 cm (½″) thick.
PLACE onto prepared baking sheet.
BAKE at 180°C (350°F) for 20-25 minutes.
Glaze:
SOFTEN Chocofix as directed on package
OR
COMBINE chocolate and butter in top of double boiler.
PLACE over boiling water stirring until smoothly melted.
DECORATE cookies with glaze.
Preparation time: approx. 50 min.
Yield: 50 cookies

Hazelnut Delights

Dough:

150 g	ground hazelnuts	1½	cups
70 g	sifted icing sugar	½	cup
1 pkg	**oetker** vanilla sugar	1	pkg.
1	egg white	1	
* 30-45 mL	rum	2-3	tbsp.
30	whole maraschino cherries	30	

Glaze:

1 pkg	**oetker** Chocofix OR	1	pkg.
100 g	semi-sweet chocolate	4	sq.
50 g	sweet (unsalted) butter	¼	cup

Decoration:

chopped candied orange peel

Dough:
CREAM nuts, icing sugar, vanilla sugar, egg white and rum together to make a smooth paste.
WRAP nut mixture around cherries, shaping into small balls.
Glaze:
SOFTEN Chocofix as directed on package
OR
COMBINE chocolate and butter in top of double boiler.
PLACE over boiling water, stirring until smoothly melted.
COVER nut balls with glaze.
DECORATE with candied orange peel.
PLACE into small paper cups.
REFRIGERATE.
Preparation time: approx. 40 min.
Yield: 30 candies

Marzipan Pyramids

Marzipan:

70 g	sifted icing sugar	½	cup
15 mL	cocoa	1	tbsp.
100 g	ground hazelnuts	1	cup
100 g	marzipan	3½	oz.
60 mL	almond liqueur or creme de cacao	¼	cup

Decoration:

hot apricot jam or marmalade
whole hazelnuts

Method:
COMBINE icing sugar, cocoa and ground hazelnuts.
ADD marzipan and liqueur.
KNEAD into a smooth paste.
SHAPE into pyramids.
DIP whole hazelnuts into hot apricot jam and place on top of pyramids.
PLACE into small paper cups.
Preparation time: approx. 40 min.
Yield: 20-30 candies

Rum Balls

100 g	ground hazelnuts	1	cup
120 g	shredded coconut	1½	cups
100 g	sweet (unsalted) butter	½	cup
100 g	sifted icing sugar	¾	cup
1 pkg	**oetker** vanilla sugar	1	pkg.
100 g	semi-sweet chocolate, grated	4	sq.
60 mL	rum	¼	cup

Decoration:

shredded coconut
sugar sprinkles
chocolate sprinkles

Method:
TOAST hazelnuts and coconut until light golden. Cool
CREAM butter. Gradually add icing sugar, vanilla sugar, chocolate and rum.
STIR in nuts and coconut to make a smooth paste.
CHILL ½ hour.
SHAPE into small balls.
ROLL in decoration.
PLACE into small paper cups.
REFRIGERATE.
Preparation time: approx. 50 min.
Yield: 40-50 rumballs

Light or Dark Chocolate Almond Chunks

200 g	chopped almonds, toasted	1⅔ cups
200 g	chocolate, white and/or semi-sweet dark chocolate	8 sq.

Method:
TOAST chopped almonds.
PUT chocolate in top of double boiler.
PLACE over boiling water, stirring until smoothly melted.
MIX toasted almonds and melted chocolate together.
COVER baking sheet with foil paper.
DROP mixture by teaspoon onto foil.
Refrigerate overnight to harden.
Preparation time: approx. 30 min.
Yield: 20 candies

Walnut Pralines

100 g	sweet (unsalted) butter	½ cup
100 g	sifted icing sugar	¾ cup
100 g	semi-sweet chocolate, grated	4 sq.
100 g	ground walnuts	1 cup

Glaze:

50 g	semi-sweet chocolate, grated	2 sq.
30 g	sweet (unsalted) butter	1 oz.

Decoration:

	walnuts

Method:
CREAM butter and icing sugar in mixer bowl till light and fluffy.
FOLD grated chocolate and nuts into mixture.
PLACE into decorating bag. Chill for 15 minutes.
SQUEEZE small mounds onto a plate.
Glaze:
COMBINE chocolate and butter in top of double boiler.
PLACE over boiling water, stirring until smoothly melted.
DECORATE with glaze and walnuts.
PLACE in small paper cups.
STORE in a cool place.
Preparation time: approx. 40 min.
Yield: 30-40 pralines

Whiskey Truffles

100 g	semi-sweet chocolate	4 sq.
50 g	milk chocolate	2 sq.
100 g	sweet (unsalted) butter	½ cup
100 g	sifted icing sugar	¾ cup
1 pkg	**oetker** vanilla sugar	1 pkg.
30 mL	cocoa	2 tbsp.
45 mL	whiskey	3 tbsp.

Decoration:

30 mL	chopped almonds or pistachios	2 tbsp.

Method:
PLACE chocolate in top of double boiler over boiling water stirring until smoothly melted.
CREAM butter, icing sugar and vanilla sugar in mixer bowl until light and fluffy. Gradually add cocoa, whiskey and melted chocolate.
PLACE mixture into decorating bag with large star tube. Chill 15 minutes.
SQUEEZE mounds into small paper cups.
DECORATE with nuts.
REFRIGERATE overnight to harden.
STORE in a cool place.
Preparation time: approx. 40 min.
Yield: 40-50 truffles

Crunchy Almond Temptation

40 g	sweet (unsalted) butter	¼	cup
100 g	chopped almonds	¾	cup
100 g	sugar	½	cup
100 g	semi-sweet chocolate	4	sq.

Decoration:

sugar pearls, optional

Method:
HEAT butter in saucepan.
TOAST almonds and sugar in butter until golden brown.
POUR out onto greased baking sheet and let cool completely.
BREAK up into small pieces. Place into a bowl.
MELT chocolate and stir into almond mixture.
DROP mixture by teaspoon into small paper cups.
DECORATE with sugar pearls if desired. Let cool.
Preparation time: approx. 40 min.
Yield: 30-40 candies

Chestnut Surprises

227 g	chestnut puree, softened	8	oz.
50 g	sifted icing sugar	½	cup
2 pkg	**oetker** vanilla sugar	2	pkg.
100 g	semi-sweet chocolate	4	sq.
100 g	butter	½	cup
30 mL	brandy	2	tbsp.

Decoration:

silver sugar pearls

Method:
COMBINE chestnut puree, icing sugar and vanilla sugar.
MELT chocolate.
STIR in butter and brandy.
ADD chestnut mixture. Mix well.
LET cool until mixture has paste-like consistency (approx. 1 hour).
FILL into decorating bag with large star tube.
PIPE into small paper cups.
DECORATE with sugar pearls.
STORE in cool place.
Preparation time: approx. 30 min.
Yield: 50-60 candies

Mocha Pralines

200 g	ground, toasted hazelnuts	2	cups
120 g	icing sugar	1	cup
1 pkg	**oetker** vanilla sugar	1	pkg.
15 mL	cocoa	1	tbsp.
45 mL	instant coffee	3	tbsp.
45 mL	hot water	3	tbsp.
15 mL	red jam or marmalade	1	tbsp.

Glaze:

2 pkg	**oetker** Chocofix OR	2	pkg.
200 g	semi-sweet chocolate	8	sq.
100 g	sweet (unsalted) butter	½	cup

Decoration:

mocha beans
white chocolate, melted

Method:
COMBINE hazelnuts, icing sugar, vanilla sugar and cocoa in mixing bowl. Stir well.
DISSOLVE instant coffee in water.
STIR into nut mixture.
ADD jam and knead into a smooth dough.
SHAPE into small balls.
Glaze:
SOFTEN Chocofix as directed on package
OR
COMBINE chocolate and butter in top of double boiler.
PLACE over boiling water, stirring constantly until smoothly melted.
COVER balls with chocolate glaze. Let glaze set.
DECORATE each ball with white chocolate and a mocha bean.
PLACE into small paper cups.
Preparation time: approx. 50 min.
Yield: 30-40 pralines

Chocolate Slices

100 g	sweet (unsalted) butter	½ cup	
100 g	semi-sweet chocolate	4 sq.	
200 g	ground almonds	2 cups	
30 g	chopped candied lemon peel	¼ cup	
30 g	slivered almonds	¼ cup	
pinch	cinnamon	pinch	
pinch	ground cloves	pinch	
30 mL	lemon juice	2 tbsp.	
1	egg, beaten	1	
100 g	sifted icing sugar	¾ cup	

Method:
COMBINE butter and chocolate in top of double boiler.
PLACE over boiling water, stirring until smoothly melted.
STIR ground almonds, lemon peel, slivered almonds, cinnamon and cloves into mixture.
ADD lemon juice and beaten egg.
KNEAD sifted icing sugar into mixture.
SHAPE into a roll.
WRAP in foil paper.
REFRIGERATE for 2-3 days to mellow flavour.
CUT into thin slices.
Preparation time: approx. 30 min.
Yield: 50-60 slices

Mocha Cubes

5	rice paper* each 20 cm (8″) square	5	

Filling:

15 g	instant coffee mix	1 tbsp.	
250 mL	whipping cream	1 cup	
250 g	semi-sweet chocolate	10 sq.	
60 mL	egg liqueur	¼ cup	

*available in European and Oriental stores

Method:
COMBINE whipping cream and coffee in small saucepan.
BREAK chocolate into small pieces. Add to whipping cream mixture. Bring to a boil. Let cool completely.
STIR in egg liqueur.
BEAT with electric mixer until stiff.
SPREAD mixture evenly onto 4 squares of rice paper.
PLACE squares on top of each other.
COVER with last square. Cover with plastic wrap.
REFRIGERATE overnight, so layers will stay together.
CUT into cubes. Refrigerate.
Preparation time: approx. 40 min.
Yield: 30-40 candies

Snowman

Batter:

200 g	butter, softened	1	cup
250 g	sugar	1¼	cups
1 pkg	**oetker** vanilla sugar	1	pkg.
5	eggs	5	
	juice of one orange		
45 mL	milk	3	tbsp.
4 g	ginger	1	tsp.
3 drops	**oetker** almond flavouring concentrate	3	drops
45 mL	cocoa	3	tbsp.
120 g	ground almonds	1¼	cups
80 g	shredded coconut	1	cup
100 g	semi-sweet chocolate, grated	4	sq.
350 g	all-purpose flour	2⅓	cups
1 pkg	**oetker** baking powder (14 g/1 tbsp.)	1	pkg.

Filling:

75 mL	strained apricot jam or marmalade	⅓	cup

Glaze:

300 g	sifted icing sugar	2½	cups
1 btl	**oetker** lemon flavouring concentrate	1	btl.
2	egg whites, lightly beaten	2	

Decoration:

melted chocolate
shredded coconut
coloured sugar flowers,
pearls etc.

Batter:
PREHEAT oven to 160°C (325°F). Grease and flour snowman shaped spring form pan.
CREAM butter, sugar and vanilla sugar in mixer bowl. Gradually add eggs, orange juice, milk, ginger, flavouring concentrate, cocoa, almonds, coconut and chocolate. Beat at medium speed until light and fluffy. SIFT flour and baking powder together. Fold in gently but thoroughly.
TURN batter into prepared pan.
BAKE on lower oven rack at 160°C (325°F) for 45-50 minutes.
REMOVE from pan. Let cool completely.
SPREAD jam thinly over entire cake.

Glaze:
COMBINE icing sugar, flavouring concentrate and enough egg white to make a smooth spreadable icing.
SPREAD glaze evenly over jam.
SQUEEZE melted chocolate onto waxed paper to shape a broom. Let cool to harden.
REMOVE from waxed paper.
DECORATE snowman with chocolate broom, coconut, chocolate and sugar shapes.

Gingerbread Tree

Batter:

100	g	butter	½ cup
200	g	liquid honey	¾ cup
75	mL	milk	⅓ cup
50	g	sugar	¼ cup
1	pkg	**oetker** vanilla sugar	1 pkg.
2		eggs	2
1	btl	**oetker** rum flavouring concentrate	1 btl.
3	drops	**oetker** almond flavouring concentrate	3 drops
4	g	cinnamon	1 tsp.
4	g	ginger	1 tsp.
2	g	ground cloves	½ tsp.
2	g	nutmeg	½ tsp.
350	g	all-purpose flour	2⅓ cups
1	pkg	**oetker** baking powder (14 g/1 tbsp.)	1 pkg.
50	g	raisins	⅓ cup
50	g	currants	⅓ cup
50	g	chopped candied orange and lemon peel	½ cup
50	g	ground nuts	½ cup

Filling:

75	mL	strained apricot jam or marmalade	⅓ cup

Glaze:

2	pkg	**oetker** Chocofix OR	2 pkg.
200	g	semi-sweet chocolate	8 sq.
100	g	sweet (unsalted) butter	½ cup

Decoration:

icing decorator (in tube)
coloured sugar pearls or candies
small candles (optional)

Batter:
PREHEAT oven to 160°C (325°F). Grease and flour Christmas tree shaped spring form pan.
COMBINE butter, honey, milk, sugar and vanilla sugar in saucepan.
HEAT until sugar is dissolved, stirring constantly.
TURN mixture into large mixer bowl. Cool slightly.
STIR eggs, flavouring concentrates, cinnamon, ginger, cloves and nutmeg into honey mixture.
SIFT flour and baking powder together.
ADD remaining ingredients to egg mixture by alternating spoonfuls of flour with raisins, currants, lemon/orange peel and ground nuts.
TURN batter into prepared baking pan.
BAKE on lower rack of oven at 160°C (325°F) for about 45 minutes.
SPREAD jam thinly over baked tree.

Glaze:
SOFTEN Chocofix as directed on package
OR
COMBINE chocolate and butter in top of double boiler.
PLACE over boiling water, stirring constantly until smoothly melted.
COVER tree with chocolate glaze. Let harden.
DECORATE with icing, coloured candies and candles as desired.

Recipe No. 228

Chocolate Train

Batter:

100 g	butter, softened	½ cup
150 g	sugar	¾ cup
1 pkg	**oetker** vanilla sugar	1 pkg.
2	eggs	2
250 g	all-purpose flour	1⅔ cups
8 g	**oetker** baking powder	2 tsp.
30 mL	cocoa	2 tbsp.
100 g	ground hazelnuts	1 cup
75 mL	milk	⅓ cup

Hazelnut Cream Filling:

100 g	sweet (unsalted) butter	½ cup
50 g	sifted icing sugar	½ cup
1	egg yolk	1
1 pkg	**oetker** vanilla sugar	1 pkg.
15 mL	hazelnut cream spread	1 tbsp.
50 g	semi-sweet chocolate, melted	2 sq.

Chocolate Glaze:

250 mL	apricot jam, heated	1 cup
2 pkg	**oetker** Chocofix OR	2 pkg.
200 g	semi-sweet chocolate	8 sq.
100 g	sweet (unsalted) butter	½ cup

Lemon Glaze:

| 50 g | sifted icing sugar | ½ cup |
| 15-30 mL | lemon juice | 1-2 tbsp. |

Batter:
PREHEAT oven to 180°C (350°F). Grease a 2 L (39 cm × 26 cm/15″ × 10″) jelly roll pan. Line with waxed paper. Grease again.
CREAM butter, sugar, vanilla sugar and eggs together until light and fluffy.
SIFT flour, baking powder and cocoa together.
STIR into creamed mixture, alternating with nuts and milk. Mix well.
SPREAD batter onto prepared baking pan.
BAKE on middle oven rack at 180°C (350°F) for 20-25 minutes.
REMOVE waxed paper immediately after baking and place cake on waxed paper sprinkled with icing sugar. Let cool.

Hazelnut Cream Filling:
COMBINE butter, icing sugar and egg yolk until light and fluffy.
STIR in vanilla sugar, hazelnut cream spread and melted chocolate.
CUT parts required for train out of baked cake. To form individual wagons, press together 2 rectangles and parts of locomotive using hazelnut cream filling as "glue" to hold parts together (see picture).
CUT out wheels for train.
ATTACH wheels to train with cream filling.
BRUSH hot apricot jam over top and sides of train.

Chocolate Glaze:
SOFTEN Chocofix as directed on package
OR
COMBINE chocolate and butter in top of double boiler.
PLACE over boiling water, stirring constantly until smoothly melted.
BRUSH over entire train. Let cool to set chocolate.

Lemon Glaze:
COMBINE icing sugar and enough lemon juice to make a smooth paste.
DECORATE train as desired.
NOTE: Use brush to apply hot jam and glaze to cake.

Christmas Wreath

Dough:

500	g	all-purpose flour	3⅓	cups	
1	pkg	**oetker** active dry yeast	1	pkg.	
pinch		salt		pinch	
100	g	sugar	½	cup	
1	pkg	**oetker** vanilla sugar	1	pkg.	
1	btl	**oetker** lemon flavouring concentrate	1	btl.	
		grated rind of lemon			
1		egg	1		
60	g	melted butter	⅓	cup	
250	mL	lukewarm milk	1	cup	
100	g	raisins	1	cup	
1		egg, lightly beaten	1		

Decoration:

100	g	almond paste	3½	oz.	
50	g	sifted icing sugar	⅓	cup	
5	mL	rose water or lemon juice	1	tsp.	
		red, green food colouring			
		whole blanched almonds			

Dough:

PREHEAT oven to 180°C (350°F). Grease a baking sheet.

MIX ¾ of the flour and yeast. Make a well in centre.

PUT salt, sugar, vanilla sugar, flavouring concentrate, lemon rind, egg, butter and milk in well.

KNEAD dough until ingredients well mixed.

KNEAD remaining ¼ flour and raisins into dough. Continue kneading until dough is smooth and no longer sticky (8-10 min.).

COVER and LET RISE in warm place for 30 minutes.

DIVIDE dough into 3 equal portions.

SHAPE dough into 3 rolls (80 cm/30" long).

BRAID the three rolls together.

SHAPE into a wreath. Seal ends together well.

PLACE on prepared baking sheet. Cover with a cloth.

LET RISE in warm place for 15-30 minutes.

BRUSH with beaten egg.

BAKE on middle oven rack at 180°C (350°F) for 30-40 minutes or until golden.

Decoration:

COMBINE almond paste, icing sugar and rose water.

KNEAD well into a smooth paste.

COLOUR ½ of almond paste mixture with red food colouring.

SHAPE into a roll.

DIVIDE into 4 rolls of equal length. Mould into candle shape.

DECORATE top of each roll with an almond (as flame for candle).

COLOUR remaining almond paste green.

ROLL out to 6 mm (¼") thickness.

CUT out star and leaf shapes.

DECORATE wreath as desired.

Santa Claus - Christmas Tree Cookies

Batter:

200 g	liquid honey	⅔	cup
75 mL	milk	5	tbsp.
100 g	sugar	½	cup
1 pkg	**oetker** vanilla sugar	1	pkg.
100 g	butter	½	cup
1	egg	1	
4 g	ginger	1	tsp.
pinch	salt		pinch
1 btl	**oetker** lemon flavouring concentrate	1	btl.
30 mL	cocoa	2	tbsp.
500 g	all-purpose flour	3⅓	cups
1 pkg	**oetker** baking powder (14 g/1 tbsp.)	1	pkg.
1	egg yolk, lightly beaten	1	

Decoration:

2 pkg	**oetker** Chocofix OR	2	pkg.
200 g	semi-sweet chocolate	8	sq.
100 g	sweet (unsalted) butter	½	cup

Sugar Glaze:

100 g	sifted icing sugar	1	cup
15-30 mL	egg white, lightly beaten	1-2	tbsp.
	food colouring		
	coloured sugar pearls		
	coloured sugar sprinkles		

Batter:

CUT Santa Claus and Christmas tree shapes out of waxed paper using stencils provided with baking book
PREHEAT oven to 180°C (350°F). Grease a baking sheet. Line with waxed paper. Grease again.
COMBINE honey, milk, sugar, vanilla sugar and butter in saucepan.
HEAT mixture slowly, stirring constantly until smoothly melted.
TURN into a mixer bowl. Cool to room temperature.
STIR egg, ginger, salt, flavouring concentrate and cocoa into honey mixture.
SIFT ⅔ of flour and baking powder together.
FOLD in gently but thoroughly.
KNEAD remaining ⅓ of flour into mixture to make a smooth dough.
ROLL out dough on prepared baking sheet to 6 mm (¼") thickness.
PLACE waxed paper patterns onto dough.
CUT out shapes as desired. Remove excess dough from around shapes.
BRUSH with beaten egg yolk.
BAKE on middle oven rack at 180°C (350°F) for 5-10 minutes or until set.
COOL completely.
Chocolate Glaze:
SOFTEN Chocofix as directed on package
OR
COMBINE chocolate and butter in top of double boiler.
PLACE over boiling water, stirring constantly until smoothly melted.
Sugar Glaze:
COMBINE sifted icing sugar and enough egg white to make a smooth spreadable icing.
COLOUR a portion of the icing with food colouring.
DECORATE shapes as desired.
Yield: approx. 2 dozen

Gingerbread House

Dough:

500 g	liquid honey	1½	cups
125 mL	water	½	cup
250 g	sugar	1¼	cups
1 pkg	**oetker** vanilla sugar	1	pkg.
	juice of one lemon		
100 g	butter	½	cup
2	eggs	2	
8 g	ginger	2	tsp.
8 g	cinnamon	2	tsp.
4 g	nutmeg	1	tsp.
4 g	cloves	1	tsp.
600 g	whole wheat flour	4	cups
600 g	rye flour	4	cups
8 g	baking soda	2	tsp.
3	egg yolks, lightly beaten	3	

Decoration:

250 g	sifted icing sugar	2	cups
1	egg white, lightly beaten	1	
	lemon juice		
	icing sugar		
	almonds		

Dough:

CUT parts of gingerbread house out of waxed paper using stencils provided with baking book.

PREHEAT oven to 160°C (325°F). Grease a baking sheet. Line with waxed paper. Grease again.

COMBINE in saucepan honey, water, sugar, vanilla sugar, lemon juice and butter. Heat, stirring constantly until smoothly melted.

TURN into a mixer bowl. Cool to room temperature.

STIR eggs and spices into mixture.

COMBINE ⅔ of flour and baking soda.

FOLD into honey mixture gently, but thoroughly.

KNEAD remaining ⅓ of flour into mixture to make a smooth dough.

ROLL out dough to 6 mm (¼″) thickness.

PLACE waxed paper pattern pieces onto dough.

CUT out shapes.

CUT floor, bricks, fence, window shutters, door and decorations out of remaining dough. Scraps of dough can be rerolled as needed.

PLACE shapes onto prepared baking sheet.

BRUSH with beaten egg yolk.

BAKE on middle oven rack at 160°C (325°F) for 8-15 minutes or until set. Time will vary with size of cookie pieces.

Sugar Glaze:

COMBINE sifted icing sugar, egg white and lemon juice to make a smooth paste.

BRUSH sugar glaze onto 'seams' of individual parts of gingerbread house.

PRESS parts together gently but firmly.

LET dry completely.

PLACE on floor part of house.

PRESS together gently. Let dry.

DECORATE as desired.

Recipe No. 232

Christmas Calendar

Dough:

250 g	liquid honey	¾ cup	
60 mL	oil	4 tbsp.	
150 g	sugar	¾ cup	
1 pkg	**oetker** vanilla sugar	1 pkg.	
1	egg	1	
4 g	cinnamon	1 tbsp.	
2 g	ground cloves	½ tsp.	
4-8 g	ginger	1-2 tsp.	
500 g	all-purpose flour	3⅓ cups	
1 pkg	**oetker** baking powder (14 g/1 tbsp.)	1 pkg.	
50 g	semi-sweet chocolate, grated	2 sq.	
100 g	ground walnuts or hazelnuts	1 cup	
1	egg yolk, lightly beaten	1	

Decoration:
Sugar Glaze:

150 g	sifted icing sugar	1⅓ cups	
30-45 mL	egg white, lightly beaten coloured sugar decorations	2-3 tbsp.	

Dough:
PREHEAT oven to 160°C (325°F). Grease a baking sheet. Line with waxed paper. Grease again.
COMBINE honey, oil, sugar and vanilla sugar in a saucepan.
HEAT mixture slowly, stirring constantly until smoothly melted.
TURN into a mixer bowl. Cool to room temperature.
STIR egg, cinnamon, cloves and ginger into mixture.
SIFT ⅔ of flour and baking powder together.
FOLD into honey mixture, alternating with grated chocolate and nuts.
KNEAD remaining ⅓ of flour into mixture to make a smooth dough.
ROLL out ¾ of dough into a rectangle 40 × 20 cm (16″ × 8″).
MARK divisions for calendar dates with a knife using stencil provided with baking book.
ROLL out remaining dough to 6 mm (¼″) thickness.
CUT out windows and doors for calendar. Press into designated areas onto calendar base.
PLACE shapes onto prepared baking sheet.
BRUSH with beaten egg yolk.
BAKE on middle oven rack at 160°C (325°F) for 20-25 minutes or until set.
Glaze:
COMBINE sifted icing sugar and enough egg white to make a thick smooth icing.
DECORATE as desired.

Angel

Dough:

500 g	all-purpose flour	3⅓	cups
180 g	sugar	¾	cup
1 pkg	**oetker** vanilla sugar	1	pkg.
1	egg	1	
1	egg yolk	1	
15 mL	milk	1	tbsp.
1 btl	**oetker** lemon flavouring concentrate	1	btl
250 g	butter, cold	1¼	cups
1	egg white, lightly beaten	1	

Lemon Glaze:

150 g	sifted icing sugar	1⅓	cups
30-45 mL	food colouring	2-3	tbsp.

Chocolate Glaze:

1 pkg	**oetker** Chocofix OR	1	pkg.
100 g	semi-sweet chocolate	4	sq.
50 g	sweet (unsalted) butter AND	¼	cup
50 g	marzipan	2	oz.
20 g	sifted icing sugar coloured sugar decorations pearls, flowers coloured icing (in tubes) strained jam	2	tbsp.

Dough:

CUT angel shapes out of waxed paper using stencils provided with baking book.

PREHEAT oven to 190°C (375°F). Grease a baking sheet. Line with waxed paper. Grease again.

SIFT flour onto a pastry board. Make a well in centre.

PUT sugar, vanilla sugar, egg, egg yolk, milk and flavouring concentrate in well. Work a little of flour into egg mixture to make a thick paste.

CUT cold butter into small pieces over flour mixture. Quickly work into flour mixture to form a smooth dough.

CHILL slightly for easy rolling.

ROLL out dough to 6 mm (¼″) thickness.

PLACE waxed paper patterns onto dough.

CUT out shapes.

PLACE onto prepared baking sheet.

BRUSH with beaten egg white.

BAKE on middle oven rack at 190°C (375°F) for 10-15 minutes or until set.

Lemon Glaze:

COMBINE icing sugar and enough lemon juice to make a thick smooth icing.

DIVIDE icing sugar mixture into several portions.

COLOUR with food colouring as desired.

Chocolate Glaze:

PREPARE Chocofix as directed on package

OR

COMBINE chocolate and butter in top of double boiler.

PLACE over boiling water, stirring constantly until smoothly melted.

COMBINE marzipan and icing sugar.

KNEAD well into a smooth paste.

COLOUR with food colouring.

DECORATE angels as desired with above glazes and decorations.

Happy New Year Bread Characters

Dough:

250 g	all-purpose flour	1⅔ cups	
1 pkg	**oetker** active dry yeast	1 pkg.	
pinch	salt	pinch	
60 g	sugar	⅓ cup	
1 pkg	**oetker** vanilla sugar	1 pkg.	
½ btl	**oetker** lemon flavouring concentrate	½ btl.	
1	egg yolk		
40 g	melted butter	¼ cup	
125 mL	lukewarm milk	½ cup	
1	egg white, lightly beaten	1	

Decoration:

currants
candied cherries
sugar sprinkles

Dough:
GREASE a baking sheet.
COMBINE flour and yeast in bowl. Make a well in centre.
PUT salt, sugar, vanilla sugar, flavouring concentrate, egg yolk, melted butter and milk in well.
KNEAD dough until ingredients are well mixed and dough is smooth and no longer sticky (8-10 min).
COVER and let rise in warm place for 30 minutes.
KNEAD again.
SHAPE dough as desired using stencils provided with baking book.
PLACE shapes onto prepared baking sheet.
COVER. LET RISE in warm place for 15-30 minutes.
BRUSH with beaten egg white.
DECORATE with currants, candied cherries and sugar sprinkles.
BAKE on middle oven rack at 160°C (325°F) for 15-20 minutes or until golden.
NOTE: DO NOT PREHEAT OVEN

Christmas Stollen

Dough:

500 g	all-purpose flour	3⅓ cups
1 pkg	**oetker** baking powder (14 g/1 tbsp.)	1 pkg.
180 g	sugar	¾ cup
1 pkg	**oetker** vanilla sugar	1 pkg.
4 drops	**oetker** almond flavouring concentrate	4 drops
5 drops	**oetker** lemon flavouring concentrate	5 drops
1 btl	**oetker** rum flavouring concentrate	1 btl.
2	eggs	2
120 g	butter, cold	⅔ cup
250 g	cream cheese or Quark	1¼ cups
200 g	raisins	1½ cups
100 g	currants	¾ cup
150 g	ground almonds	1½ cups
100 g	chopped candied orange and lemon peel	1 cup
50 g	melted butter	¼ cup

Decoration:

50 g	sifted icing sugar	½ cup

Dough:
PREHEAT oven to 160°C (325°F). Grease a 2 L (39 cm × 26 cm/15″ × 10″) jelly roll pan.
SIFT flour and baking powder together onto pastry board. Make a well in centre.
PUT sugar, vanilla sugar, flavouring concentrates and eggs in well.
WORK a little flour into egg mixture to make a thick paste.
CUT cold butter into small pieces over flour mixture.
KNEAD butter, cream cheese, fruit and nuts into mixture to make a smooth dough. If dough is sticky add a little flour.
SHAPE into a loaf on prepared baking pan.
BAKE on middle oven rack at 160°C (325°F) for 50-60 minutes or until golden.
BRUSH cake immediately after baking with melted butter.
SPRINKLE with icing sugar before serving.

Braided Almond Loaf

Dough:

500 g	all-purpose flour	3⅓ cups
1 pkg	**oetker** active dry yeast	1 pkg.
pinch	salt	pinch
80 g	sugar	⅓ cup
1 pkg	**oetker** vanilla sugar	1 pkg.
½ btl	**oetker** lemon flavouring concentrate	½ btl.
1	egg	1
50 g	melted butter	¼ cup
250 mL	lukewarm milk	1 cup

Filling:

180 g	marzipan	6 oz.
30 g	sifted icing sugar	¼ cup
150 g	ground almonds	1½ cups
1	egg white, lightly beaten	1
30 mL	rum	2 tbsp.
30 mL	milk	2 tbsp.
1	egg yolk, lightly beaten	1
5 mL	milk	1 tsp.

Dough:
GREASE a baking sheet.
COMBINE flour and yeast in large bowl. Make a well in centre.
PUT salt, sugar, vanilla sugar, flavouring concentrate, egg, butter and milk in well. Mix ingredients to a smooth dough. Knead dough until it is smooth and no longer sticky (8-10 min).
COVER and LET RISE in warm place for 45 minutes.
Filling:
COMBINE marzipan, icing sugar, ground almonds, egg white, rum and milk.
WORK into a smooth paste.
ROLL out dough to 1 cm (⅓″) thickness on lightly floured surface.
SPREAD filling evenly on dough.
ROLL up dough starting with a corner.
MAKE lengthwise cuts with a sharp knife 3 cm (1¼″) deep.
TWIST dough roll so that cut area is turned to upper side (see picture).
PLACE dough on prepared baking sheet.
LET RISE, covered, in warm place for 30 minutes.
COMBINE egg yolk and milk.
BRUSH dough with egg mixture.
BAKE on middle oven rack at 200°C (400°F) for 30-40 minutes or until golden.

New Year's Eve Cake

Batter:

220	g	butter, softened	1	cup
220	g	sugar	1	cup
1	pkg	**oetker** vanilla sugar	1	pkg.
4		eggs	4	
500	g	all-purpose flour	3⅓	cups
1	pkg	**oetker** baking powder (14 g/1 tbsp.)	1	pkg.
125	mL	milk	½	cup
45	mL	cocoa	3	tbsp.
15	mL	sugar	1	tbsp.
30-45	mL	water	2-3	tbsp.
100-120	mL	rum about	½	cup

Filling:

125	mL	strained red currant jam or marmalade	½	cup

Glaze:

2	pkg	**oetker** Chocofix OR	2	pkg.
200	g	semi-sweet chocolate	8	sq.
100	g	sweet (unsalted) butter	½	cup

Decoration:

100	g	marzipan	3	oz.
50	g	sifted icing sugar food colouring	½	cup

Lemon Glaze:

50	g	sifted icing sugar lemon juice	½	cup

Batter:
PREHEAT oven to 160°C (325°F). Grease and flour 3 baking pans 24 cm/9½″ diameter that are each divided in three ring sections.
CREAM butter. Gradually add sugar, vanilla sugar and eggs together until light and fluffy.
SIFT flour and baking powder together.
STIR into creamed mixture, alternating with milk.
DIVIDE mixture into 2 equal portions.
COMBINE cocoa, sugar and water until smooth.
MIX thoroughly into one portion of batter.
TURN batter into prepared baking pan as follows: Turn dark batter into outside ring and centre section of 2 baking pans, filling second ring of each pan with light batter. Turn light batter into outside ring and centre of third pan and dark batter into centre section of third pan.
BAKE on middle oven rack at 160°C (325°F) for 20-25 min.
REMOVE from pans immediately and sprinkle rum on cakes.
Spread jam over top of cakes.
PLACE cake with dark outside ring on serving plate. Place cake with white outside ring on top. Press together carefully.
COVER with third cake.
SPREAD sides of cake with jam.
Glaze:
SOFTEN Chocofix as directed on package OR
COMBINE chocolate and butter in top of double boiler.
PLACE over boiling water, stirring constantly until smoothly melted.
SPREAD glaze evenly over top and sides of cake.
Decoration:
KNEAD marzipan and icing sugar until smooth.
COLOUR with food colouring.
SHAPE into different forms (see picture).
Lemon Glaze:
COMBINE sifted icing sugar and enough lemon juice to make a smooth paste.
DECORATE cake as desired.

Chestnut Cream Pyramid

125	mL	red wine	½	cup
50	g	sugar	¼	cup
1		cinnamon stick	1	
3		whole cloves	3	
150	g	lady fingers	18	

Cream Filling:

150	g	butter, softened	¾	cup
80	g	sugar	⅓	cup
1	pkg	**oetker** vanilla sugar	1	pkg.
100	g	semi-sweet chocolate	4	sq.
45	mL	whipping cream	3	tbsp.
100	g	chestnut pureé, softened	3½	oz.
45	mL	red wine	3	tbsp.
1		egg yolk	1	

Decoration:

250	mL	whipping cream	1	cup
1	pkg	**oetker** Whip it	1	pkg.
1	pkg	**oetker** vanilla sugar	1	pkg.
50	g	semi-sweet chocolate, melted coloured sugar decorations	2	sq.

Method:
COMBINE red wine, sugar, cinnamon stick and cloves in saucepan. Bring to a boil. Let cool.
SOAK lady fingers in wine mixture.
CREAM butter, sugar and vanilla sugar until light and fluffy.
MELT chocolate.
STIR whipping cream into chocolate and let cool.
FOLD chocolate mixture into butter mixture.
STIR chestnut pureé, red wine and egg yolk into creamed mixture.
ARRANGE layer of lady fingers on cake plate to form bottom of pyramid (2 × 3 lengthwise).
SPREAD evenly with some of filling.
COVER with a row of (2 × 2) lady fingers.
SPREAD evenly with filling.
COVER with another row of (2 × 1) lady fingers (top of pyramid).
Decoration:
BEAT whipping cream to soft peaks. Gradually add Whip it and vanilla sugar, beating to stiff peaks.
SPREAD sides of pyramid with remaining chestnut cream filling.
COVER with lady fingers cut in half.
DECORATE with whipped cream and lady fingers dipped in melted chocolate and coloured sugar decorations.

Christmas Log

Batter:

50 g	butter, softened	¼	cup
100 g	sugar	½	cup
1 pkg	**oetker** vanilla sugar	1	pkg.
5	egg yolks	5	
50 g	semi-sweet chocolate, grated	2	sq.
15 mL	cocoa	1	tbsp.
5 mL	cinnamon	1	tsp.
30 mL	brandy	2	tbsp.
100 g	ground almonds	1	cup
30 g	dry bread crumbs	½	cup
2 g	**oetker** baking powder	½	tsp.
5	egg whites	5	

Glaze:

60 mL	red current jelly	¼	cup
80 g	semi-sweet chocolate	3	sq.
40 g	sweet (unsalted) butter	¼	cup

Decoration:

125 mL	whipping cream	½	cup
1 pkg	**oetker** vanilla sugar chocolate stars	1	pkg.

Batter:
PREHEAT oven to 180°C (350°F). Grease an elegant shaped loaf pan. Sprinkle with bread crumbs.
CREAM butter, sugar and vanilla sugar in mixer bowl.
Gradually add egg yolks, grated chocolate, cocoa, cinnamon and brandy. Beat at high speed of electric mixer until thick and creamy.
MIX almonds, bread crumbs and baking powder together. Fold into egg mixture gently, but thoroughly.
BEAT egg whites to stiff peaks.
FOLD egg whites gently into egg yolk mixture.
TURN batter into prepared pan.
BAKE on lower rack of oven at 180°C (350°F) for 45-50 minutes.
REMOVE from pan immediately.
SPREAD with red currant jelly. Cool.

Glaze:
COMBINE chocolate and butter in top of double boiler. Place over boiling water, stirring constantly until smooth melted.
SPREAD quickly over top and sides of cake.
BEAT whipping cream to soft peaks. Gradually add vanilla sugar, beating to stiff peaks.
PLACE in decorating bag.
DECORATE chocolate loaf attractively with whipped cream and chocolate stars.

Advent Hazelnut Loaf

Dough:

350 g	all-purpose flour	2⅓	cups
1 pkg	**oetker** instant dry yeast	1	pkg.
50 g	sugar	¼	cup
1 pkg	**oetker** vanilla sugar	1	pkg.
pinch	salt		pinch
½ btl	**oetker** lemon flavouring concentrate	½	btl.
1	egg	1	
50 g	melted butter	¼	cup
125 mL	lukewarm milk	½	cup

Filling:

200 g	ground hazelnuts	2	cups
1	egg white	1	
80 g	sugar	⅓	cup
1 pkg	**oetker** vanilla sugar	1	pkg.
4 g	cinnamon	1	tsp.
15 mL	apricot jam or marmalade	1	tbsp.
½ btl	**oetker** rum flavouring concentrate	½	btl.
1	egg yolk, beaten	1	
5 mL	milk	1	tsp.

Dough:
GREASE a baking sheet.
COMBINE flour and yeast in large bowl. Make a well in centre.
PUT sugar, vanilla sugar, salt, flavouring concentrate, egg, melted butter and milk in well.
MIX ingredients working from centre.
KNEAD dough until smooth, elastic and no longer sticky (8-10 min).
LET RISE covered in a warm place for 30 minutes.

Filling:
COMBINE hazelnuts, egg white, sugar, vanilla sugar, cinnamon, jam and flavouring concentrate, mixing until smooth.
ROLL out bread dough to a rectangle 30 × 40 cm (12" × 16").
SPREAD filling on centre part of rectangle 8 cm (3") wide.
CUT dough into strips 2 cm (¾") wide on a slight angle on both sides of the filling.
FOLD strips over filling, alternating sides to form loaf (see picture). Press ends of loaf lightly together to seal.
PLACE loaf onto prepared baking sheet. Cover.
LET RISE in a warm place for 30 minutes.
BRUSH with mixture of egg yolk and milk.
PRICK loaf in several places with toothpick or fork.
BAKE on lower oven rack at 180°C (350°F) for 25-35 minutes or until golden.
NOTE: Do NOT preheat oven.

Nut Bundt Cake

Batter:

150 g	butter, softened	¾	cup
150 g	sugar	¾	cup
1 pkg	**oetker** vanilla sugar	1	pkg.
5	egg yolks	5	
45 mL	brandy	3	tbsp.
1 btl	**oetker** lemon flavouring concentrate	1	btl.
150 g	all-purpose flour	1	cup
8 g	**oetker** baking powder	2	tsp.
150 g	ground almonds	1½	cups
100 g	chopped hazelnuts	1	cup
100 g	semi-sweet chocolate, chopped	4	sq.
100 g	raisins	⅔	cup
5	egg whites	5	
60 mL	strained apricot jam or marmalade	¼	cup

Glaze:

100 g	sifted icing sugar	¾	cup
4 g	cinnamon	1	tsp.
15-30 mL	water	1-2	tbsp.

Decoration:

coloured sugar shapes

Batter:
PREHEAT oven to 180°C (350°F). Grease and flour 24 cm (9½") bundt pan.
CREAM butter, ⅔ of sugar and vanilla sugar in mixer bowl. Gradually add egg yolks, brandy and flavouring concentrate.
BEAT at high speed until light and fluffy.
COMBINE flour, baking powder, ground almonds, hazelnuts, chocolate and raisins. Add to creamed mixture.
BEAT egg whites to soft peaks. Gradually add remaining ⅓ of sugar beating to stiff peaks.
FOLD egg whites into creamed mixture, gently but thoroughly.
TURN batter into prepared pan.
BAKE on lower oven rack at 180°C (350°F) for 50-55 minutes.
REMOVE cake from pan immediately.
SPREAD apricot jam over hot cake. Cool.
Glaze:
COMBINE icing sugar, cinnamon and water, stirring until smooth.
SPREAD evenly over cake.
DECORATE with sugar shapes.

Gingerbread Diamonds

Batter:

400 g	liquid honey	1¼	cups
100 g	sugar	½	cup
1 pkg	**oetker** vanilla sugar	1	pkg.
100 g	butter	½	cup
3	eggs	3	
pinch	salt	pinch	
5-10 mL	cinnamon	1-2	tsp.
pinch	ground cloves	pinch	
pinch	nutmeg	pinch	
400 g	all-purpose flour	2⅔	cups
1 pkg	**oetker** baking powder (14 g/1 tbsp.)	1	pkg.
100 g	ground nuts	1	cup
50 g	chopped, candied lemon peel	½	cup
50 g	chopped, candied orange peel	½	cup

Decoration:

4 pkg	**oetker** Chocofix OR	4	pkg.
400 g	semi-sweet chocolate	16	sq.
200 g	sweet (unsalted) butter almonds	1	cup

Batter:
PREHEAT oven to 180°C (350°F). Grease a 2 L (39 cm × 26 cm/15" × 10") jelly roll pan.
COMBINE honey, sugar, vanilla sugar and butter in saucepan.
HEAT mixture slowly, stirring constantly until smoothly melted.
TURN into a mixer bowl. Cool to room temperature.
STIR in eggs, salt, cinnamon, cloves and nutmeg.
SIFT flour and baking powder together.
FOLD into egg mixture.
ADD nuts and candied peels.
SPREAD batter evenly in prepared pan.
BAKE on middle oven rack at 180°C (350°F) for 30-40 minutes.
LET cool.
CUT into diamond shapes.
Glaze:
SOFTEN Chocofix as directed on package
OR
COMBINE chocolate and butter in top of double boiler.
PLACE over boiling water, stirring constantly until smoothly melted.
DECORATE diamonds with chocolate glaze and almonds.

Christmas Star

Batter:

150 g	almond paste, softened	6	oz.
80 g	butter	⅓	cup
150 g	sugar	¾	cup
1 pkg	**oetker** vanilla sugar	1	pkg.
4	eggs	4	
pinch	salt		pinch
1 btl	**oetker** rum flavouring concentrate	1	btl.
50 g	ground walnuts or hazelnuts	½	cup
50 g	semi-sweet chocolate, grated	2	sq.
200 g	all-purpose flour	1⅓	cups
4 g	**oetker** baking powder	1	tsp.
45 mL	strained apricot jam or marmalade	3	tbsp.

Glaze:

2 pkg	**oetker** Chocofix OR	2	pkg.
200 g	semi-sweet chocolate	8	sq.
100 g	sweet (unsalted) butter	½	cup

Praline:

50 g	chopped almonds	½	cup
20 g	butter	2	tbsp.
50 g	sugar	¼	cup

Caramel Sticks:

20 g	butter	2	tbsp.
50 g	sugar	¼	cup

Decoration:

125 mL	whipping cream	½	cup

Batter:
PREHEAT oven to 180°C (350°F). Grease and flour a star shaped pan.
CUT almond paste into small pieces.
COMBINE almond paste and butter in mixer bowl. Beat until a smooth paste. Gradually add sugar, vanilla sugar, eggs, salt, flavouring concentrate, nuts and grated chocolate.
SIFT flour and baking powder together.
FOLD in gently but thoroughly.
TURN batter into prepared baking pan.
BAKE on lower oven rack at 180°C (350°F) for 30-40 minutes.
REMOVE from pan immediately.
SPREAD apricot jam over top and sides of hot cake.

Glaze:
PREPARE Chocofix according to package directions OR
COMBINE chocolate and butter in top of double boiler. Place over boiling water, stirring constantly until smoothly melted.
SPREAD over sides and top of cake.

Praline:
COOK almonds in butter and sugar in a saucepan until caramelized. Pour onto a greased baking sheet. Let cool.
CRUSH into small pieces.

Caramel Sticks:
COOK butter and sugar in saucepan until golden. ROLL up foil paper to form thin rolls.
SPREAD hot butter and sugar mixture over foil paper rolls. Let cool.
REMOVE carefully from foil paper.
WHIP cream to stiff peaks.
DECORATE cake attractively with whipped cream, crushed praline and caramel sticks.

Recipe No. 244

Fruit Cake

Dough:
250 g	rye flour	1⅔	cups
200 g	whole wheat flour	1⅓	cup
1 pkg	**oetker** instant dry yeast	1	pkg.
6 g	salt	1	tsp.
4 g	anise	1	tsp.
40 g	sugar	¼	cup
40 g	melted butter	¼	cup
250 mL	lukewarm milk	1	cup
1	egg, lightly beaten	1	

Filling:
120 g	dried pears	1	cup
500 mL	water	2	cups
100 g	pitted prunes	1	cup
120 g	figs	1¼	cups
80 g	raisins	⅔	cup
50 g	chopped candied orange peel	½	cup
50 g	chopped candied lemon peel	½	cup
	grated rind of 1 lemon		
	grated rind of 1 orange		
4 g	cinnamon	1	tsp.
2 g	ground cloves	½	tsp.
60 mL	rum	¼	cup
50 g	pine nuts	½	cup
50 g	chopped almonds	½	cup
50 g	chopped hazelnuts	½	cup
50 g	chopped walnuts	½	cup

Decoration:
whole blanched almonds

Filling: *Prepare the day before.*
COOK pears in saucepan with water for 25 minutes or until tender. Strain, save water.
CHOP pears.
COOK prunes in same water until all water thickens.
CUT prunes and figs into small strips.
COMBINE pears, prunes, figs, raisins, candied peels, lemon and orange rind, cinnamon, cloves and rum in bowl.
COVER. Let stand overnight.
STIR in all nuts.

Dough:
GREASE a baking sheet. Line with waxed paper. Grease again.
COMBINE ¾ of flour and yeast in large bowl. Make well in centre.
PUT salt, anise, sugar, melted butter and milk in well. Working from centre, stir until all ingredients are well blended.
KNEAD remaining ¼ of flour into mixture until dough is smooth and no longer sticky.
LET RISE, covered in warm place for about 40 minutes.
DIVIDE dough into 2 equal portions.
FOLD filling into one portion of dough. Mix gently, but thoroughly.
SHAPE into a roll.
ROLL out remaining dough on floured surface to a rectangular shape.
BRUSH beaten egg onto dough.
PLACE dough with filling on top and wrap plain dough around filling mixture.
PLACE onto prepared baking sheet.
LET RISE, covered in warm place for 20-30 minutes.
BRUSH with beaten egg.
PIERCE several times with a fork.
DECORATE with almonds.
BAKE on middle oven rack at 180°C (350°F) for 35-40 minutes or until golden.

Chocolate Strudel

Dough:

250 g	all-purpose flour	1⅔ cups
15 mL	lemon juice	1 tbsp.
30 mL	oil	2 tbsp.
pinch	salt	pinch
150 mL	lukewarm water	⅔ cup

Filling:

80 g	butter, softened	⅓ cup
80 g	sugar	⅓ cup
1 pkg	**oetker** vanilla sugar	1 pkg.
3	egg yolks	3
½ btl	**oetker** rum flavouring concentrate	½ btl.
125 mL	whipping cream	½ cup
70 g	ground hazelnuts	¾ cup
80 g	bread crumbs	¾ cup
100 g	semi-sweet chocolate, grated	4 sq.
100 g	raisins	¾ cup
3	egg whites	3
80 g	melted butter or margarine	⅓ cup
250 mL	hot milk	1 cup

Chocolate Sauce:

1 L	milk	4 cups
100 g	sugar	½ cup
4 pkg	**oetker** chocolate sauce mix	4 pkg.
1 pkg	**oetker** vanilla sugar	1 pkg.
30 mL	rum	2 tbsp.

Dough:

PREHEAT oven to 200°C (400°F). Grease a large baking pan.
SIFT flour onto pastry board. Make a well in centre.
PUT lemon juice, oil, salt and water in well.
COMBINE ingredients mixing from centre with a fork, adding enough water to make a stiff dough.
WORK dough until smooth, shiny and blistered in appearance.
SHAPE dough into a small loaf.
BRUSH lightly with oil.
COVER with a thick cloth and let rest for 1 hour.
PLACE a linen tablecloth over a large table. Sprinkle with flour.
ROLL out dough thinly on cloth, then start to pull the dough to stretch it by putting it over the back of your hands and gently pulling outward in all directions.
Stretch dough as thin as possible. Cut off thick edges.

Filling:

CREAM butter, ⅔ of sugar and vanilla sugar in mixer bowl. Gradually add egg yolks, flavouring concentrate and whipping cream.
BEAT at medium speed until light and fluffy.
STIR in nuts, bread crumbs, chocolate and raisins.
BEAT egg whites to soft peaks. Gradually add remaining ⅓ of sugar beating to stiff peaks.
FOLD egg whites gently but thoroughly into creamed mixture.
BRUSH melted butter over dough.
SPREAD filling over ½ of dough.
ROLL up tightly starting at end with filling, using tablecloth to help roll.
PLACE in prepared baking pan.
BRUSH lightly with melted butter.
BAKE on lower oven rack at 200°C (400°F) for 40-45 minutes or until crisp and golden.
AFTER 15 minutes baking time, slowly pour hot milk over strudel into baking pan.

Chocolate Sauce:

PREPARE chocolate sauce mix according to directions on package. Gradually stir in vanilla sugar and rum.
CUT strudel into serving pieces and serve with chocolate sauce.

Recipe No. 246

Christmas Poppy Seed Stollen from Cologne

Dough:

450 g	all-purpose flour	3	cups
1 pkg	**oetker** instant dry yeast	1	pkg.
3 g	salt	½	tsp.
100 g	sugar	½	cup
1 pkg	**oetker** vanilla sugar	1	pkg.
2	eggs	2	
150 g	melted butter	¾	cup
125 mL	lukewarm milk	½	cup
50 g	chopped almonds	½	cup

Filling:

250 mL	milk	1	cup
150 g	ground poppy seeds	1	cup
50 g	ground nuts	½	cup
1 pkg	**oetker** vanilla pudding mix	1	pkg.
100 g	sugar	½	cup
1 pkg	**oetker** vanilla sugar	1	pkg.
20 g	bread crumbs	¼	cup
1	egg yolk	1	
1	egg white, lightly beaten	1	

Glaze:

200 g	sifted icing sugar	1½	cups
	juice of 1 lemon		

Decoration:

30 g	toasted sliced almonds	⅓	cup

Dough:

GREASE a 2 L (39 cm × 26 cm/15" × 10") jelly roll pan. Line with waxed paper. Grease again.
COMBINE flour and yeast in large bowl. Make a well in centre.
PUT salt, sugar, vanilla sugar, eggs, butter and milk in well.
KNEAD all ingredients together to make a smooth dough. Lastly knead almonds into dough.
LET RISE covered in warm place for 30 minutes.

Filling:

COMBINE ¾ of milk, ground poppy seeds and nuts in saucepan. Bring to a boil. Remove from heat.
COMBINE vanilla pudding mix and remaining ¼ of milk.
STIR into poppy seed mixture. Bring to a boil, stirring constantly.
ADD sugar, vanilla sugar, bread crumbs and egg yolk. Mix well. Cool completely.
ROLL out dough on lightly floured surface to a rectangle (25 cm × 60 cm/10" × 24".)
SPREAD filling evenly over dough.
ROLL up starting from both sides simultaneously so that rolls meet in centre.
PLACE dough on prepared baking pan.
LET RISE again for about 15 minutes.
BAKE on middle oven rack at 180°C (350°F) for 30-40 minutes or until golden.

Glaze:

COMBINE sifted icing sugar and enough lemon juice to make a smooth glaze consistency.
SPREAD over top and sides of baked loaf.
SPRINKLE with toasted sliced almonds.

Chocolate Loaf

Batter:

180 g	sweet (unsalted) butter, softened	¾ cup	
150 g	sugar	¾ cup	
1 pkg	**oetker** vanilla sugar	1 pkg.	
3	eggs	3	
5 drops	**oetker** rum flavouring concentrate	5 drops	
180 g	all-purpose flour	1¼ cup	
4 g	**oetker** baking powder	1 tsp.	
15 mL	cocoa	1 tbsp.	
30 g	pistachios	¼ cup	

Filling:

60 mL	strained apricot jam or marmalade	¼ cup	

Glaze:

90 g	sifted icing sugar	⅔ cup	
10 g	cocoa	1 tsp.	
30-45 mL	hot water	2-3 tbsp.	

Decoration:

shaved chocolate
chopped pistachios

Batter:
PREHEAT oven to 180°C (350°F). Grease and flour a loaf pan.
CREAM butter, sugar and vanilla sugar in mixer bowl. Gradually add eggs and flavouring concentrate.
BEAT at high speed until light and fluffy.
SIFT flour, baking powder and cocoa together over creamed mixture. Stir well.
ADD pistachios.
TURN batter into prepared pan.
BAKE on lower oven rack at 180°C (350°F) for 40-50 minutes.
REMOVE from pan immediately.
SPREAD with apricot jam while hot. COOL.
Glaze:
BLEND sifted icing sugar, cocoa and enough hot water t
make a smooth glaze consistency.
SPREAD over cake.
DECORATE with shaved chocolate and pistachios.

Gingerbread Slices

Batter:

150 g	butter, softened	¾ cup	
250 g	sugar	1¼ cups	
1 pkg	**oetker** vanilla sugar	1 pkg.	
4	eggs	4	
375 g	all-purpose flour	2½ cups	
8 g	**oetker** baking powder	2 tsp.	
4 g	ginger	1 tsp.	
2 g	cinnamon	½ tsp.	
pinch	cloves	pinch	
pinch	nutmeg	pinch	
200 mL	milk	¾ cup	
50 g	chopped hazelnuts	½ cup	
50 g	raisins	½ cup	

Filling:

125 mL	hot apricot jam or marmalade	½ cup	

Lemon Glaze:

100 g	sifted icing sugar	¾ cup	
15-30 mL	lemon juice	1-2 tbsp.	

Chocolate Glaze:

1 pkg	**oetker** Chocofix OR	1 pkg.	
100 g	semi-sweet chocolate	4 sq.	
50 g	sweet (unsalted) butter	¼ cup	

Batter:
PREHEAT oven to 190°C (375°F). Grease a 2 L (39 cm × 26 cm/15″ × 10″) jelly roll pan.
CREAM butter, sugar, vanilla sugar and eggs together thoroughly.
SIFT flour, baking powder and spices together.
ADD to creamed mixture alternately with milk.
STIR in nuts and raisins.
TURN batter into prepared pan spreading evenly.
BAKE on middle oven rack at 190°C (375°F) for 15-20 minutes. Let cool.
SPREAD cake with jam.
CUT in half lengthwise. Put halves together.
CUT into strips.
Lemon Glaze:
BLEND sifted icing sugar and enough lemon juice together to make a smooth glaze consistency.
Chocolate Glaze:
SOFTEN Chocofix as directed on package
OR
COMBINE chocolate and butter in top of double boiler.
PLACE over boiling water, stirring constantly until smoothly melted.
DECORATE slices with lemon and chocolate glaze.

Fruit Loaf

*Sourdough:

125	mL	lukewarm water	½ cup
100	g	rye flour	⅔ cup

Filling:

500	mL	water	2 cups
250	g	dried pears	9 oz.
250	g	dried prunes (pitted)	9 oz.
250	g	figs	9 oz.
250	g	chopped walnuts or hazelnuts	9 oz.

Dough:

300	g	rye flour	2 cups
200	g	whole wheat flour	1⅓ cups
100	g	sourdough*	3½ oz.
1	pkg	**oetker** instant dry yeast	1 pkg.
	pinch	salt	pinch
4	g	cinnamon	1 tsp.
4	g	ground cloves	1 tsp.
45	mL	liquid honey	3 tbsp.
45	mL	rum	3 tbsp.
250	mL	lukewarm pear juice water	1 cup

*Sourdough: *Prepare several days in advance.*
COMBINE water and ½ of the rye flour.
LET REST, covered, in a warm place for several days until mixture begins to ferment.
ADD remaining flour.
LET REST for 1 hour.
Filling:
SOAK dried pears overnight in water.
BRING to a boil and simmer for 30 minutes. (Put aside 250 mL (1 cup) of pear juice for dough).
CHOP pears, dried prunes and figs coarsely.
Dough:
GREASE a baking sheet.
MIX ¾ of flour in large bowl. Make a well in centre.
PUT sour dough, yeast, salt, cinnamon, cloves, honey, rum and pear juice into well.
KNEAD dough until smooth and elastic (8-10 min).
ADD remaining flour. Knead until dough is smooth and no longer sticky.
LET RISE covered in a warm place for 1 hour.
PUNCH down. Add fruit and nuts.
KNEAD again until fruit is well mixed into dough.
DIVIDE dough into two portions and shape each into a loaf or a braid.
PLACE onto prepared baking sheet.
LET RISE for 30 minutes.
BRUSH lightly with water.
BAKE on middle oven rack at 180°C (350°F) for 60-75 minutes.
*Prepared sourdough can be purchased in some bakeries.

Christmas Angel Macaroon Torte

Dough (Base):

80	g	all-purpose flour	½	cup
40	g	sugar	3	tbsp.
1	pkg	**oetker** vanilla sugar	1	pkg.
1		egg yolk	1	
50	g	butter, cold	¼	cup
75	mL	strained red currant jam or marmalade	⅓	cup

Macaroon Cake:

6		egg whites	6	
pinch		salt	pinch	
160	g	icing sugar	1⅓	cup
60	g	all-purpose flour	⅓	cup
100	g	ground hazelnuts	1	cup
½	btl	**oetker** lemon flavouring concentrate	½	btl.
50	mL	brandy	¼	cup

Filling:

250	mL	whipping cream	1	cup
1	pkg	**oetker** Whip it	1	pkg.
1	pkg	**oetker** vanilla sugar	1	pkg.

Decoration:

250	g	marzipan	9	oz.
100	g	sifted icing sugar	1	cup
1		egg yolk	1	
30	mL	lemon juice	2	tbsp.
50	g	toasted, sliced almonds	½	cup
		food colouring		
		coloured sugar shots		
		melted chocolate		

Dough (Base):

PREHEAT oven to 180°C (350°F). Grease a baking sheet and line with waxed paper. Grease again.
SIFT flour onto a pastry board. Make a well in centre
PLACE sugar, vanilla sugar and egg yolk in well.
Work some of the flour into centre to make a thick paste.
CUT cold butter into small pieces over flour mixture.
WORK all ingredients together quickly into a smooth dough.
CHILL slightly for easy rolling (about ½ hour).
ROLL out on baking sheet to a 24 cm (9½") circle.
Trim edges if necessary.
BAKE on middle oven rack at 180°C (350°F) for 10-15 minutes.
SPREAD top of cake with jam.

Macaroon Cake:

PREHEAT oven to 160°C (325°F). Grease a 24 cm (9½") spring form pan, line with waxed paper. Grease again.
BEAT egg whites and salt to soft peaks. Gradually add icing sugar, beating until very stiff.
FOLD in flour, nuts and lemon flavouring concentrate
TURN mixture into prepared baking pan.
BAKE on lower oven rack at 160°C (325°F) for 30-35 minutes. Let cool.
CUT horizontally to make 2 layers.
SPRINKLE with brandy.

Filling and Assembly:

BEAT whipping cream to soft peaks. Gradually add Whip it and vanilla sugar, beating until stiff.
COVER base with one layer of macaroon cake.
COVER with ⅓ of whipped cream.
PLACE second macaroon layer over whipped cream.
SPREAD remaining ⅔ whipped cream over sides and top of cake.

Decoration:

KNEAD marzipan, icing sugar, egg yolk and lemon juice together into a smooth paste.
DIVIDE into 2 equal portions.
ROLL out one portion to a circle 24 cm (9½") diameter.
COVER cake with marzipan layer.
DECORATE sides of cake with toasted, sliced almonds.
COLOUR part of remaining marzipan (see picture).
SHAPE almond paste into stars, angels, leaves etc.
DECORATE as desired with marzipan shapes, coloured sugar and melted chocolate.

Recipe No. 251

Burgundy Torte

Batter:

4	egg yolks	4
100 g	sugar	½ cup
1 pkg	**oetker** vanilla sugar	1 pkg.
4	egg whites	4
80 g	all-purpose flour	½ cup
4 g	**oetker** baking powder	1 tsp.
1 pkg	**oetker** chocolate pudding mix	1 pkg.

Filling:

1 pkg	**oetker** gelatine, clear	1 pkg.
250 mL	red wine (burgundy)	1 cup
120 g	sugar	⅔ cup
1 pkg	**oetker** vanilla sugar	1 pkg.
	juice of ½ lemon	
250 mL	whipping cream	1 cup

Chocolate Glaze:

80 g	semi-sweet chocolate	3 sq.
50 g	sweet (unsalted) butter	¼ cup
125 mL	whipping cream	½ cup
½ pkg	**oetker** Whip it	½ pkg.

Batter:
PREHEAT oven to 160°C (325°F). Grease a 24 cm (9½″) spring form pan. Line with waxed paper. Grease again.
COMBINE egg yolks, ⅔ of sugar and vanilla sugar.
BEAT at high speed of electric mixer until thick and creamy.
BEAT egg whites and remaining sugar to stiff peaks.
FOLD into egg yolk mixture gently.
SIFT flour, baking powder and pudding mix together over egg mixture. Fold in gently.
TURN batter into prepared pan.
BAKE on lower oven rack at 160°C (325°F) for 35-40 minutes.
REMOVE from pan immediately and let cake cool completely. Clean pan.
SLICE cake horizontally with thread to make 2 layers.
PLACE bottom layer in cleaned spring form pan.
Filling:
COMBINE gelatine, wine, sugar, vanilla sugar and lemon juice in saucepan.
HEAT, stirring constantly until completely dissolved (DO NOT BOIL). Let cool until gelatine starts to set.
BEAT whipping cream to stiff peaks.
FOLD whipped cream gently into slightly jelled gelatine mixture.
SPREAD gelatine filling on bottom cake layer.
COVER with top cake layer. Chill until set.
REMOVE spring form rim carefully.
Chocolate Glaze:
COMBINE chocolate and butter in top of double boiler. Place over boiling water, stirring constantly until smoothly melted.
SPREAD quickly over top and sides of torte.
BEAT whipping cream to soft peaks. Gradually add Whip it, beating to stiff peaks.
DECORATE torte attractively with whipped cream.

Christmas Rum Cream Torte

Batter:

5	eggs	5
150 g	sugar	¾ cup
1 pkg	**oetker** vanilla sugar	1 pkg.
½ btl	**oetker** rum flavouring concentrate	½ btl.
200 g	all-purpose flour	1⅓ cups
pinch	**oetker** baking powder	pinch

Filling:

500 mL	whipping cream	2 cups
50 g	sugar	¼ cup
1 pkg	**oetker** Whip it	1 pkg.
2 pkg	**oetker** vanilla sugar	2 pkg.
30 mL	cocoa	2 tbsp.
30 mL	rum	2 tbsp.
1 pkg	**oetker** vanilla sugar	1 pkg.
60 mL	lingonberry, cherry or raspberry jam	4 tbsp.

Decoration:

50 g	semi-sweet chocolate	2 sq.
100 g	chocolate sprinkles cocoa	1 cup

Batter:

PREHEAT oven to 180°C (350°F). Grease a 24 cm (9½″) spring form pan.

COMBINE eggs, sugar, vanilla sugar and rum flavouring concentrate in mixer bowl.

BEAT at high speed of electric mixer until thick and creamy.

SIFT flour and baking powder together over egg mixture.

FOLD in gently but thoroughly.

TURN batter into prepared pan.

BAKE on lower oven rack at 180°C (350°F) for 35-40 minutes.

REMOVE from pan immediately and let cake cool completely.

SLICE cake horizontally to make 3 even layers.

Filling and Assembly:

BEAT whipping cream to soft peaks. Gradually add sugar, Whip it and vanilla sugar, beating to stiff peaks. Divide into 4 equal portions.

COMBINE cocoa, rum and vanilla sugar.

FOLD into one portion of whipped cream mixture.

SPREAD on bottom cake layer.

COVER with second cake layer.

FOLD jam into second portion of whipped cream mixture.

SPREAD over second cake layer.

COVER with third cake layer.

SPREAD third portion of whipped cream mixture over top and sides of torte.

MELT chocolate in double boiler.

SPREAD thinly onto waxed paper. Let harden.

CUT out half moons and bells.

DECORATE torte attractively with remaining whipped cream and chocolate shapes.

DUST lightly with cocoa.

Recipe No. 253

Poppy Seed Torte

Batter:

150	g	butter	¾ cup
150	g	sugar	¾ cup
1	pkg	**oetker** vanilla sugar	1 pkg.
4		egg yolks	4
1	btl	**oetker** lemon flavouring concentrate	1 btl.
2	g	cinnamon	½ tsp.
45	mL	milk	3 tbsp.
150	g	ground poppy seeds	1 cup
1	pkg	**oetker** vanilla pudding	1 pkg.
4		egg whites	4
80	g	all-purpose flour	½ cup
4	g	**oetker** baking powder	1 tsp.
125	mL	strained red currant jam	½ tbsp.

Lemon Glaze:

150	g	sifted icing sugar	1½ cups
30-45	mL	lemon juice	2-3 tbsp.

Decoration:

50	g	toasted, sliced almonds	½ cup
		poppy seeds	

Batter:
PREHEAT oven to 180°C (350°F). Grease a 24 cm (9½″) spring form pan.
CREAM butter in mixer bowl. Gradually add ⅔ of sugar, vanilla sugar, egg yolks, flavouring concentrate, cinnamon, milk, poppy seeds and pudding powder.
BEAT at medium speed until light and fluffy.
BEAT egg whites and remaining sugar to stiff peaks.
FOLD into egg yolk mixture gently.
SIFT flour and baking powder together over egg mixture. Fold in gently.
TURN batter into prepared pan.
BAKE on lower rack at 180°C (350°F) for 35-40 min.
REMOVE from pan immediately and let cake cool.
SLICE cake horizontally to make 2 layers.
SPREAD jam on bottom cake layer.
COVER with top cake layer.
SPREAD jam over top and sides of cake.
Lemon Glaze:
COMBINE sifted icing sugar and enough lemon juice to make a smooth spreading consistency.
SPREAD over top and sides of cake.
SPRINKLE sides with almonds and top with poppy seeds.

Recipe No. 254

Aunt Mary's Chocolate Torte

Batter:

150	g	butter	¾ cup
4		egg yolks	4
150	g	sugar	¾ cup
1	pkg	**oetker** vanilla sugar	1 pkg.
1	btl	**oetker** rum flavouring concentrate	1 btl.
200	g	all-purpose flour	1⅓ cups
45	mL	cocoa	3 tbsp.
8	g	**oetker** baking powder	2 tsp.
60	mL	milk	4 tbsp.
4		egg whites	4
125	mL	strained red currant jam or marmalade	½ cup

Filling:

250	mL	whipping cream	1 cup
1	pkg	**oetker** Whip it	1 pkg.
1	pkg	**oetker** vanilla sugar	1 pkg.
50	g	semi-sweet chocolate, grated	2 sq.

Glaze:

80	g	semi-sweet chocolate, dark	3 sq.
80	g	semi-sweet chocolate, white	3 sq.
60	g	shortening	⅓ cup

Batter:
PREHEAT oven to 180°C (350°F). Grease a 24 cm (9½″) spring form pan. Line with waxed paper. Grease again.
CREAM butter in mixer bowl. Gradually add egg yolks, ⅔ of sugar, vanilla sugar and flavouring concentrate. Beat at medium speed until light and fluffy.
SIFT flour, cocoa and baking powder together.
FOLD into egg mixture alternating with milk.
BEAT egg whites and remaining sugar to stiff peaks.
FOLD egg whites gently into egg yolk mixture.
TURN batter into prepared pan.
BAKE on lower oven rack at 180°C (350°F) for 30-35 minutes.
REMOVE from pan immediately. Let cake cool.
SLICE cake horizontally to make 2 layers.
SPREAD bottom cake layer thinly with some of the jam.
Filling:
BEAT whipping cream to soft peaks. Gradually add Whip it and vanilla sugar, beating until stiff.
FOLD in grated chocolate.
SPREAD filling evenly over jam on bottom cake layer.
COVER with second cake layer.
SPREAD top and sides of torte with remaining jam.
Glaze:
COMBINE dark chocolate and ½ of shortening in top of double boiler. Place over boiling water, stirring constantly until smoothly melted.
REPEAT same procedure for white chocolate and remaining shortening.
SAVE a little for decoration and spread remaining dark and white chocolate quickly over top and sides of torte, forming marble pattern (see picture).
SPREAD thin layer of the reserved white and dark chocolate onto foil paper. Let harden. Break into pieces.
DECORATE torte with chocolate pieces.

IABETICS

Kiwi Cheesecake for Diabetics

Batter:

2	egg yolks	2
75 mL	water	⅓ cup
75 mL	oil	⅓ cup
	juice of 1 lemon	
100 g	fruit sugar	⅔ cup
2	egg whites	2
150 g	all-purpose flour	1 cup
4 g	**oetker** baking powder	1 tsp.

Cheese Filling:

500 g	low-fat cottage cheese or Quark	2½ cups
2	egg yolks	2
100 g	fruit sugar	⅔ cup
1 pkg	**oetker** gelatine, clear	1 pkg.
	juice of 1 lemon	
80 g	jam or marmalade for diabetics	3 oz.

Decoration:

30 g	toasted, sliced almonds	⅓ cup
100 g	kiwis, sliced	3½ oz.
20 g	jam or marmalade for diabetics	¾ oz.

Batter:
PREHEAT oven to 180°C (350°F). Grease a 24 cm (9½″) spring form pan.
CREAM egg yolks and water in mixer bowl. Gradually add oil, lemon juice and sugar. Beat until light and fluffy.
BEAT egg whites to stiff peaks.
SIFT flour and baking powder together over egg yolk mixture. Fold in gently but thoroughly.
FOLD in egg whites gently.
TURN batter into prepared pan.
BAKE on lower oven rack at 180°C (350°F) for 25-30 minutes.
REMOVE from pan. Let cake cool completely.

Cheese Filling:
COMBINE cottage cheese, egg yolks and sugar. Mix together until smooth.
HEAT (DO NOT BOIL) gelatine and lemon juice in saucepan until completely dissolved.
STIR into cheese mixture.
SPREAD side and top of cake with jam.
REPLACE rim of spring form pan on cake.
SPREAD cottage cheese mixture evenly over cake.
REFRIGERATE for several hours until set.
REMOVE spring form rim carefully.
SPRINKLE toasted, sliced almonds over sides of cake.
DECORATE with kiwi and jam.
Yield: 12 servings

Exchanges per serving: 2 milk choices + 1½ starchy food choices

Per serving:	Calories	Kilojoules	Carbohydrate	Protein	Fat
(¹⁄₁₂ of cheesecake)	250	1038	33.0g	10g	9.2g

Honey Cookies for Diabetics

Dough:

170	g	honey for diabetics	½	cup
50	g	fruit sugar	⅓	cup
	pinch	salt		pinch
30	mL	oil	2	tbsp.
45	mL	water	3	tbsp.
1		egg yolk	1	
6	drops	**oetker** lemon flavouring concentrate	6	drops
4	g	cinnamon	1	tsp.
1	g	cloves	¼	tsp.
200	g	all-purpose flour	1⅓	cups
1	pkg	**oetker** baking powder (14 g/1 tbsp.)	1	pkg.
10	g	cocoa	1	tbsp.
150	g	ground hazelnuts	1½	cups

Filling:

120	g	jam or marmalade for diabetics	4	oz.

Glaze:

80	g	chocolate for diabetics	3	oz.
30	g	butter	1	oz.

Dough:

PREHEAT oven to 160°C (325°F). Grease a baking sheet. Line with waxed paper. Grease again.

COMBINE in saucepan honey, sugar, salt, oil and water. Heat up slowly stirring, until well blended. Let cool.

ADD egg yolk, lemon flavouring concentrate, cinnamon and cloves to mixture.

SIFT flour, baking powder and cocoa together.

STIR ⅔ of flour mixture into honey mixture, blending thoroughly. Knead remaining flour mixture and nuts into mixture to make a smooth dough.

ROLL out thinly on lightly floured surface.

CUT into 5 cm (2″) rounds with cookie cutter.

PLACE onto prepared baking sheet.

BAKE on middle oven rack at 160°C (325°F) for 8-10 minutes.

LET cool completely.

SPREAD jam on half the cookies. Place other half of cookies on top of jam. Press together lightly.

Glaze:

COMBINE chocolate and butter in top of double boiler. Place over boiling water, stirring constantly until smoothly melted.

DIP cookies into chocolate glaze for decoration. Place on rack over waxed paper until chocolate sets.

STORE in airtight container for two weeks together with an apple to make cookies chewy if desired.

Preparation time: approx. 50 min.

Yield: 40-50 cookies

Exchanges per serving: ½ starchy food choice + 1 fat choice

Per serving:	Calories	Kilojoules	Carbohydrate	Protein	Fat
(1 cookie)	79	330.7	9.3g	1.21g	4.1g

Butter Cookies for Diabetics

Dough:

150 g	all-purpose flour	1 cup	
1 g	**oetker** baking powder	¼ tsp.	
pinch	salt	pinch	
50 g	fruit sugar	⅓ cup	
5 drops	**oetker** lemon flavouring concentrate	5 drops	
1	egg	1	
50 g	butter, cold	¼ cup	

Glaze:

50 g	chocolate for diabetics	2 oz.	
20 g	butter	¾ oz.	

Decoration:

60 g	jam or marmalade for diabetics	2 oz.	

Dough:
PREHEAT oven to 180°C (350°F). Grease a baking sheet. Line with waxed paper. Grease again.
SIFT flour and baking powder together onto pastry board. Make a well in centre.
PUT salt, sugar, flavouring concentrate and egg in well.
CUT cold butter into small pieces over mixture.
WORK all ingredients together quickly into a smooth dough.
CHILL for easy rolling (about ½ hour).
ROLL out dough thinly on lightly floured surface.
CUT out desired shapes with floured cookie cutters.
PLACE on prepared baking sheet.
BAKE on middle oven rack at 180°C (350°F) for 5-8 minutes. Cool.

Glaze:
COMBINE chocolate and butter in top of double boiler. Place over boiling water, stirring constantly until smoothly melted.
DECORATE cookies with chocolate glaze and jam.
Preparation time: approx. 60 min.
Yield: 30-40 cookies

Exchanges per serving: ½ starchy food choice + ½ fat choice

Per serving:	Calories	Kilojoules	Carbohydrate	Protein	Fat
(1 cookie)	48	201.6	5.36g	0.8g	2.4g

Almond Macaroons for Diabetics

Dough:

50 g	butter	¼ cup	
100 g	fruit sugar	⅔ cup	
2 drops	**oetker** almond flavouring concentrate	2 drops	
1	egg	1	
100 g	shredded coconut	1 cup	
150 g	ground almonds	1½ cups	

Method:
PREHEAT oven to 150°C (300°F). Grease a baking sheet. Line with waxed paper.
CREAM butter in mixer bowl. Gradually add sugar, flavouring concentrate and egg.
BEAT at medium speed until light and fluffy.
STIR coconut and almonds into mixture.
PLACE dough by small spoonfuls onto prepared baking sheet.
BAKE on middle oven rack at 150°C (300°F) for 10-12 minutes.
Preparation time: approx 40 min.
Yield: 50-60 cookies

Exchanges per serving: ½ starchy food choice + 1 fat choice

Per serving:	Calories	Kilojoules	Carbohydrate	Protein	Fat
(2 cookies)	75	312	5.0g	1.4g	5.0g

Nut Delights for Diabetics

Dough:

50 g	fruit sugar	⅓ cup	
15 mL	rose water	1 tbsp.	
40 g	jam or marmalade for diabetics	1½ oz.	
100 g	ground hazelnuts	1 cup	

Glaze:

80 g	chocolate for diabetics	3 oz.	
30 g	butter	1 oz.	

Decoration:

chopped walnuts

Dough:
CREAM fruit sugar, rose water and jam together to make a smooth paste.
STIR in ground hazelnuts.
SHAPE into small balls.
Glaze:
COMBINE chocolate and butter in top of double boiler.
PLACE over boiling water, stirring until smoothly melted.
COVER nut balls with glaze.
DECORATE with chopped walnuts.
PLACE into small paper cups. Let set.
REFRIGERATE.
Preparation time: approx. 40 min.
Yield: 20 cookies

Exchanges per serving: ½ starchy food choice + 1 fat choice

Per serving:	Calories	Kilojoules	Carbohydrate	Protein	Fat
(1 cookie)	88	371	4.85g	1.15g	6.85g

Chocolate Cookies for Diabetics

Dough:

60 g	butter	2 oz.	
100 g	fruit sugar	⅔ cup	
2	eggs	2	
5 drops	**oetker** lemon flavouring concentrate	5 drops	
20 g	cocoa	1 oz.	
250 g	all-purpose flour	1⅔ cups	
8 g	**oetker** baking powder	2 tsp.	

Filling:

300 g	jam or marmalade for diabetics	10 oz.	

Glaze:

50 g	chocolate for diabetics	2 oz.	
30 g	butter	¾ oz.	

Dough:
PREHEAT oven to 180°C (350°F). Grease a baking sheet. Line with waxed paper. Grease again.
CREAM butter in mixer bowl. Gradually add sugar, eggs, flavouring concentrate and cocoa. Beat at medium speed until light and fluffy.
SIFT flour and baking powder together.
STIR ⅔ of flour mixture into egg mixture, blending thoroughly.
KNEAD remaining flour into mixture to make a smooth dough.
REFRIGERATE for ½ hour for easy rolling.
ROLL out thinly on lightly floured surface.
CUT out desired shapes with cookie cutters.
PLACE onto prepared baking sheet.
BAKE on middle oven rack at 180°C (350°F) for 8-10 minutes.
LET cool completely.
SPREAD jam on half the cookies. Cover with remaining cookies. Press lightly together.
Glaze:
COMBINE chocolate and butter in top of double boiler. Place over boiling water, stirring constantly until smoothly melted.
DECORATE cookies with chocolate glaze.
Preparation time: approx. 50 min.
Yield: 40-50 cookies

Exchanges per serving: ½ starchy food choice + ½ fat choice

Per serving:	Calories	Kilojoules	Carbohydrate	Protein	Fat
(1 cookie)	63	264.3	9.3g	1.1g	2.3g

Chocolate Spritz Cookies for Diabetics

Dough:

150 g	butter	¾ cup	
100 g	fruit sugar	⅔ cup	
	grated rind of 1 orange		
2	eggs	2	
50 g	grated chocolate for diabetics	2 sq.	
150 g	all-purpose flour	1 cup	

Glaze:

50 g	chocolate for diabetics	2 sq.	
20 g	butter	¾ oz.	

Dough:
PREHEAT oven to 150°C (300°F). Grease a baking sheet. Line with waxed paper. Grease again.
CREAM butter in mixer bowl. Gradually add sugar, orange rind, eggs and chocolate.
BEAT at medium speed until light and fluffy.
SIFT flour over creamed mixture. Mix well.
PUT mixture into decorating bag with large star tube.
SQUEEZE onto prepared baking sheet in desired shapes.
BAKE on middle oven rack at 150°C (300°F) for 15 minutes.

Glaze:
COMBINE chocolate and butter in top of double boiler.
PLACE over boiling water, stirring constantly until smoothly melted.
DECORATE cookies with chocolate glaze.
Preparation time: approx. 50 min.
Yield: 30-40 cookies

Exchanges per serving: ½ starchy food choice + 1 fat choice

Per serving:	Calories	Kilojoules	Carbohydrate	Protein	Fat
(1 cookie)	80	334	6.3g	1.1g	5.1g

Poppy Seed Rounds for Diabetics

Dough:

150 g	all-purpose flour	1 cup	
60 g	fruit sugar	½ cup	
20 g	ground poppy seeds	1 oz.	
20 mL	milk	4 tsp.	
60 g	butter, cold	2 oz.	

Filling:

100 g	strained jam or marmalade for diabetics	3½ oz.	

Decoration:

20 g	strained jam or marmalade for diabetics poppy seeds	1 oz.	

Dough:
PREHEAT oven to 180°C (350°F). Grease a baking sheet. Line with waxed paper. Grease again.
SIFT flour on a pastry board. Make a well in centre.
PUT sugar, poppy seeds and milk in well. Mix small amount of flour into centre ingredients to make a thick paste.
CUT cold butter into small pieces over flour mixture. Working quickly from centre, work all ingredients to make a smooth dough.
IF dough is sticky, chill slightly for easy handling (about ½ hour).
ROLL out dough thinly on lightly floured surface.
CUT into 5 cm (2″) rounds with cookie cutter.
PLACE on prepared baking sheet.
BAKE on middle oven rack at 180°C (350°F) for 8-10 minutes.
LET COOL completely.
SPREAD jam over half the cookies. Cover with remaining cookies. Press slightly together.
DECORATE with jam and poppy seeds.
Preparation time: approx. 50 min.
Yield: 20-30 cookies

Exchanges per serving: ½ starchy food choice + ½ fat choice

Per serving:	Calories	Kilojoules	Carbohydrate	Protein	Fat
(1 cookie)	60	250	8.6g	0.76g	1.84g

Marble Bundt Cake

Batter:

200 g	butter, softened	1 cup
300 g	liquid honey	1 cup
5	eggs	5
	juice of 1 lemon	
300 g	whole wheat flour	2 cups
1 pkg	**oetker** baking powder (14 g/1 tbsp.)	1 pkg.
100 g	ground almonds	1 cup
45 mL	cocoa	3 tbsp.
4 g	cinnamon	1 tsp.
90 mL	milk	6 tbsp.

Decoration:

sifted icing sugar

Batter:
PREHEAT oven to 180°C (350°F). Grease and flour 24 cm (9½") bundt pan.
CREAM butter in mixer bowl. Gradually add honey, eggs and lemon juice.
BEAT at medium speed until light and fluffy.
COMBINE flour and baking powder. Add to creamed mixture.
STIR in almonds. Mix well.
TURN ⅔ of batter into prepared pan.
STIR cocoa, cinnamon and milk into remaining batter.
SPREAD dark batter over light batter in pan.
DRAW a fork through both mixtures and swirl the two together to create marble effect.
BAKE on lower oven rack at 180°C (350°F) for 40-45 minutes.
REMOVE from pan and let cake cool completely.
SPRINKLE with icing sugar.

Nut Loaf

Batter:

150 g	butter, softened	¾ cup
4	egg yolks	4
100 g	brown sugar	½ cup
1 pkg	**oetker** vanilla sugar	1 pkg.
	juice of 1 lemon	
250 g	whole wheat flour	1⅔ cups
1 pkg	**oetker** baking powder (14 g/1 tbsp.)	1 pkg.
100 g	ground walnuts	1 cup
4	egg whites	4

Filling:

50 mL	jam	¼ cup
	sifted icing sugar	

Batter:
PREHEAT oven to 180°C (350°F). Grease and flour a loaf pan.
CREAM butter in mixer bowl. Gradually add egg yolks, brown sugar, vanilla sugar and lemon juice.
BEAT at medium speed until light and fluffy.
COMBINE flour and baking powder. Add to creamed mixture.
STIR in nuts. Mix well.
BEAT egg whites to stiff peaks.
FOLD egg whites gently into egg yolk mixture.
TURN batter into prepared pan.
BAKE on lower oven rack at 180°C (350°F) for 35-40 minutes.
REMOVE cake from pan and let cool completely.
CUT horizontally to make 2 layers.
SPREAD bottom cake layer with jam.
COVER with top cake layer.
SPRINKLE with icing sugar.

Coconut Swirl Cookies

Dough:

150 g	Quark or ricotta cheese	¾ cup
30 mL	liquid honey	2 tbsp.
30 mL	milk	2 tbsp.
30 mL	vegetable oil	2 tbsp.
pinch	salt	pinch
200 g	whole wheat flour	1⅓ cups
8 g	**oetker** baking powder	2 tsp.

Filling:

100 g	shredded coconut	1¼ cups
15 mL	cocoa	1 tbsp.
30 mL	liquid honey	2 tbsp.
1	egg white	1
50 g	raisins	½ cup
1	egg yolk, beaten	1

Lemon Glaze (optional):

100 g	sifted icing sugar	1 cup
15-30 mL	lemon juice	1-2 tbsp.

Dough:
PREHEAT oven to 180°C (350°F). Grease a baking sheet. Line with waxed paper. Grease again.
COMBINE cheese, honey, milk, oil and salt. Stir until smoothly blended.
COMBINE flour and baking powder. Beat ⅔ of flour mixture into cheese mixture.
KNEAD remaining flour into dough.
ROLL out dough on floured board to a 20 cm × 30 cm (8″ × 12″) rectangle.
Filling:
COMBINE coconut, cocoa, honey, egg white and raisins.
STIR until well blended.
SPREAD filling evenly over dough.
ROLL up dough jelly-roll fashion starting with longer side.
BRUSH with beaten egg yolk.
CUT into 5 mm (¼″) thick slices.
PLACE on prepared baking sheet.
BAKE on middle oven rack at 180°C (350°F) for 10-15 minutes or until golden.
Lemon Glaze (optional):
COMBINE sifted icing sugar and enough lemon juice to make a smooth glaze consistency.
DECORATE cookies with lemon glaze as desired.
Preparation time: approx. 50 min.
Yield: 40-50 cookies

Fruit Turnovers

Dough:

100 g	butter, softened	½ cup
20 g	brown sugar	2 tbsp.
1	egg	1
150 g	whole wheat flour	1 cup
100 g	ground almonds	1 cup

Filling:

50 g	chopped dried apricots	½ cup
20 g	chopped candied orange peel	¼ cup
20 g	chopped candied lemon peel	¼ cup
20 g	raisins	¼ cup
50 g	ground almonds	½ cup
30 mL	liquid honey	2 tbsp.
½ btl	**oetker** lemon flavouring concentrate	½ btl.

Glaze:

	milk	

Dough:
PREHEAT oven to 160°C (325°F). Grease a baking sheet. Line with waxed paper. Grease again.
CREAM butter. Gradually add brown sugar and egg.
ADD ⅔ of flour and ground almonds to mixture.
KNEAD remaining flour into dough.
CHILL 1 hour for easy rolling.
ROLL out dough thinly on floured surface.
CUT into 6 cm (2¼″) rounds.
Filling:
COMBINE all ingredients. Mix well.
PLACE small amount of filling on each cookie round.
FOLD in half. Press seams to seal well.
PLACE on prepared baking sheet.
BRUSH with milk.
BAKE on middle oven rack at 160°C (325°F) for 18-25 minutes or until golden.
Preparation time: approx. 40 min.
Yield: 20-30 cookies

Recipe No. 267

Chocolate Hearts

Dough:

120 g	butter	⅔ cup	
200 g	liquid honey	⅔ cup	
2	eggs	2	
100 g	semi-sweet chocolate, grated	4 sq.	
200 g	rye flour	1⅓ cups	
150 g	whole wheat flour	1 cup	
1 pkg	**oetker** baking powder (14 g/1 tbsp.)	1 pkg.	

Decoration:

2 pkg	**oetker** Chocofix OR	2 pkg.	
200 g	semi-sweet chocolate	8 sq.	
100 g	sweet (unsalted) butter	½ cup	

Dough:
PREHEAT oven to 160°C (325°F). Grease a baking sheet. Line with waxed paper. Grease again.
CREAM butter. Gradually add honey, eggs and chocolate.
BEAT at medium speed until light and fluffy.
COMBINE flours and baking powder.
STIR ⅔ of flour mixture into creamed mixture.
KNEAD remaining flour into dough.
CHILL for 30 minutes for easy rolling.
ROLL out dough on floured surface to 6 mm (¼")
thickness.
CUT out heart shapes (2 sizes).
PLACE onto prepared baking sheet.
BAKE on middle oven rack at 160°C (325°F) for 10 minutes.
Glaze:
SOFTEN Chocofix as directed on package
OR
COMBINE chocolate and butter in top of double boiler.
PLACE over boiling water, stirring constantly until smoothly melted.
DECORATE cookies as desired.
SUGGESTION: Place small cookies onto large size cookie. Press together with chocolate glaze.
Yield: 70-80 cookies

Recipe No. 268

Raspberry Rings

Dough:

100 g	butter, softened	½ cup	
100 g	liquid honey	⅓ cup	
1	egg	1	
15 mL	cinnamon	1 tbsp.	
pinch	ground cloves	pinch	
	grated rind and juice of ½ lemon		
150 g	ground hazelnuts	1½ cups	
200 g	whole wheat flour	1⅓ cups	
4 g	**oetker** baking powder	1 tsp.	

Filling:

125 mL	strained raspberry jam or marmalade	½ cup	

Dough:
PREHEAT oven to 160°C (325°F). Grease a baking sheet. Line with waxed paper. Grease again.
CREAM butter. Gradually add honey, egg, cinnamon, ground cloves, lemon juice and rind.
BEAT at medium speed until light and fluffy.
COMBINE hazelnuts, whole wheat flour and baking powder.
STIR ⅔ of flour mixture into creamed mixture.
KNEAD remaining flour mixture into dough.
CHILL for 30 minutes for easy rolling.
ROLL out on floured surface to 6 mm (¼") thickness.
CUT in 5 cm (2") rounds and rings.
PLACE rings over rounds.
PLACE on prepared baking sheet.
SPREAD jam in centre of rings.
BAKE on middle oven rack at 160°C (325°F) for 10-15 minutes. Cool completely.
Preparation time: approx. 60 min.
Yield: 30-40 cookies

Cheese Triangles

Dough:

100 g	butter	½	cup
30-45 mL	sour cream	2-3	tbsp.
100 g	grated Emmenthal or Swiss cheese	½	cup
100 g	whole wheat flour	⅔	cup
100 g	rye flour	⅔	cup

Decoration:

	paprika		
50 g	grated Emmenthal or Swiss cheese	¼	cup

Dough:

PREHEAT oven to 160°C (325°F). Grease a baking sheet. Line with waxed paper. Grease again.
COMBINE butter, sour cream, cheese and ⅔ of flour. Mix well.
KNEAD remaining flour into dough.
CHILL for 1 hour.
ROLL out on floured board to 6 mm (¼″) thickness.
SPRINKLE with paprika and grated cheese.
CUT out triangles.
PLACE triangles onto prepared baking sheet.
BAKE on middle oven rack for 160°C (325°F) for 20-25 minutes or until golden.
Preparation time: approx. 60 min.
Yield: 60-70 triangles

Caraway Rings

Dough:

200 g	whole wheat flour	1⅓	cups
½ pkg	**oetker** instant dry yeast	½	pkg.
pinch	salt		pinch
15 mL	brown sugar	1	tbsp.
4 g	ground caraway	1	tsp.
30 g	melted butter	2	tbsp.
125 mL	lukewarm milk	½	cup

For Brushing:

1	egg, lightly beaten	1

Decoration:

	caraway seeds

Dough:

Grease baking sheet. Line with waxed paper. Grease again.
COMBINE flour, yeast and salt in large bowl. Make a well in centre.
PUT sugar, caraway, melted butter and milk in well.
KNEAD into a smooth dough.
LET RISE covered in warm place for 30 minutes.
ROLL out on floured surface to 6 mm (¼″) thickness.
CUT out ring shapes.
BRUSH with beaten egg.
SPRINKLE with caraway seeds.
PLACE onto prepared baking sheet.
LET RISE covered in warm place for 20 minutes.
BAKE on middle oven rack at 160°C (325°F) for 10-15 minutes or until golden.
Preparation time: approx. 50 min.
Yield: 40-50 rings

Tips for proper storage of your Christmas baking

Christmas and baking go hand in hand! Here are a f
ideas and suggestions to help your baked goods ret
their maximum freshness.

Let all baked goods — cookies, breads and cakes cc
completely after baking before storing.
An airtight container or cookie jar will prevent drying c
of your baked goods and will keep undesirable arom
from spoiling their taste.
Always store cookies of one type together or types th
are compatible in flavour and aroma. Separate each ty
with foil or plastic wrap to help prevent breakage.

No Christmas should be without fruit bread, stollen
gingerbread. When wrapped tightly in plastic wrap or f
paper, these cakes will retain their freshness for up to fo
weeks and even improve their delicate aroma.

Macaroons: Should still feel soft to the touch aft
baking. They will still harden while cooling and mellc
during storage.

Gingerbread cookies: Stored together with orange
tangerine peel will take on a special delicate arom
flavour and texture.

Candies and pralines: Should be stored in small pap
cups which will prevent the individual pieces fro
sticking together.

Store all Christmas baked goods in a cool dry place.

A variety of Christmas cookies packaged in a colourful tin, cookie jar or wrapped attractively in clear plastic and tied with a red or green ribbon, are always a welcome gift.

HAPPY BAKING!

Recipe Index

Notes

Notes

Notes

Notes

Notes

Notes

Notes

Notes